Three Second Fighter

The sniper option

Geoff Thompson

summersdale

Summersdale Publishers Ltd
46 West Street
Chichester
West Sussex
PO19 1RP
UK

www.summersdale.com
www.geoffthompson.com

Printed and bound in Great Britain by 4edge Ltd, Hockley.

ISBN 1 84024 459 3

Other books by Geoff Thompson:

Watch My Back

Red Mist

Shape Shifter

The Elephant and the Twig

The Great Escape

A Book for the Seriously Stressed

Fear – The Friend of Exceptional People

The Throws & Take-downs of Judo

The Throws & Take-downs of Sombo

The Throws & Take-downs of Free-Style Wrestling

The Throws & Take-downs of Greco-Roman Wrestling

Animal Day

The Art of Fighting Without Fighting

Dead Or Alive – The Choice is Yours

The Fence

The Pavement Arena

Real Head, Knees and Elbows

Real Grappling

Real Kicking

Real Punching

Weight Training for the Martial Artist

Pins: The Bedrock

The Escapes

Chokes and Strangles

Fighting from Your Back

Fighting from Your Knees

Arm Bars and Joint Locks

Martial Arts DVDs by Geoff Thompson

The Method Series
The Fence
Three Second Fighter
Animal Day Part 1
Animal Day Part 2
The Pavement Arena Part 1
The Pavement Arena Part 2
The Pavement Arena Part 3
The Pavement Arena Part 4

The Real Punching Series
Real Punching-The One Punch Kill
Real Punching-Intermediate
Real Punching-Advanced

The Ground Fighting Series
Pins
Escapes
Chokes & Strangles
Armbars & Locks
Fighting From Your Back
Fighting From Your Knees
Advanced Chokes & Strangles
Advanced Armbars & Locks
Advanced Fighting From Your Back

The Throws and Takedowns
Judo Basic
Judo Intermediate
Freestyle Wrestling-Basic
Freestyle Wrestling-Intermediate
Greco Roman Wrestling
Russian Wrestling

About the author

Geoff Thompson claims that his biological birthdate is 1960, though his hair-line goes right back to the First World War.

He has worked as a floor sweeper, chemical worker, pizza maker, road digger, hod carrier, martial-arts instructor, bricklayer, picture seller, delivery driver and nightclub bouncer before giving up 'proper work' in 1992 to write full time.

He is now a bestselling author, BAFTA-nominated screenwriter, magazine columnist, playwright and novelist.

He lives in Coventry with his wife Sharon, and holds a 6th dan in Japanese karate, 1st dan in Judo and was voted the number one self-defence author in the world by *Black Belt Magazine* USA.

Contents

Foreword

Before you start reading this piece (thank you for taking the time) I'd like to make it clear that the following views are my opinion, born from experience in the world of reality, and not intended to insult or debase other martial arts or artists. I have a great love and deep respect for all the arts, so if somewhere within the next 24,000 words I do offend then you have my unreserved apology right now. I am not a politician, neither do I use my writing as a podium for biased opinion; what I am, however, is a realist. I'm honest and emphatic. Honesty often has an inadvertent habit of offending. So please read with an open and honest mind and if what I have to say helps then great, if not then you've lost nothing but the short time it takes to read.

We all have something to teach and we all have something to learn. It takes a very enlightened person to realise and accept what he lacks, but it takes a very brave person to do something about it.

Much has been said of late, in conversation and in print, about ultimate fighting arts, ultimate being the operative word used mainly to sell copy as opposed to art.

The Collins GEM English Dictionary informs us that Ultimate is 'the final in a series or process; highest or most significant'. I have even been guilty of using the word myself in a bid to better peddle my wares.

What most fail to realise is that all arts are ultimate in their own arena.

In the western boxing ring, with boxing rules, the pugilist is, no doubt, the ultimate combatant; in the arena of Olympic Wrestling - with wrestling rules - the grappler is potentate and in the Thai boxing ring - with Thai rules of course - the Thai fighter comes away with the accolade.

If, however, you put a wrestler in the boxing ring with boxing rules, the wrestler will come a very sorry second place, and vice versa, but that doesn't make the boxer any better than the wrestler or the wrestler any better than the boxer, not at all. What it does make them is the best in their own field and to their own rules. I do not look for, neither am I interested in, who is the best fighter. What I do look for and I definitely am interested in is what can I learn from the boxer/wrestler/Thai boxer/Wing Chun man etc.

I had a friend, a very capable boxer of professional standard, who fought in the ring, at his insistence, to boxing rules with a brilliant international Karataka, a phenomenal kicker who should remain nameless. Not surprisingly, the boxer tore the kicker a new arse. Afterwards he couldn't wait to tell me what an easy fight he'd had and what a poor fighter the karataka had been, as though fighting a man entwined in rules meant anything at all. I have absolutely no doubt at all that had this particular boxer fought the same karataka in the dojo - to karate rules - the boxer would have been taken completely off the planet in seconds and would probably have needed an operation to remove the kicker's foot from his stomach.

Although the Karate man lost the fight in the boxing ring I had more respect for him than the boxer, he'd gone in to a foreign arena severely impeded by rules and regulations and 'had a go' in a search for the grail of improvement.

I told the boxer this and said that I'd have a lot more respect for him if he'd displayed the same courage as the karataka and fought him at a dojo and not in a ring. Sadly my friend missed the point; all his ego would allow him to see was his embryonic victory. With this conquest (I use the word reluctantly) he lost all respect for Karate as a fighting art. After all, he surmised, if he had beaten this international player with such ease, how much simpler would an average Karate man would be? In his victory he learned nothing.

Three Second Fighter

A couple of years later the same boxer ventured into my club to box with one of my students, a capable boxer with a heavy background in traditional Karate. At the start of the fight they fought full contact and to boxing rules. There was no doubting the ferocity and prowess of the boxer's hands: he was brilliant. Although my student fought a hard and brave fight he was catching some heavy bombs. After a few rounds of boxing, and with the consent of both fighters, I changed the rules slightly and allowed the use of kicking. Within a minute the boxer had been on the floor more times than the cleaner's mop and was incapable of carrying on. My student had used only one kick to reach this end - a Thai leg kick. The boxer came to see me a week later, still limping, and told me that he hadn't been able to attend work for a week and was absolutely amazed at how effective the kicker was. This day, in his defeat, he learned many valuable lessons that could not have been taught any other way, not least always to respect exponents of every art and that, in our own arena, we are all kings.

I have also witnessed good street fighters being trounced in the controlled arena by average trained fighters who have said to me afterwards 'I thought he was supposed to be a good street fighter!'

What many of these people fail to recognise is that to deny a karataka kicking, a boxer punching, a wrestler wrestling or a street fighter street fighting etc is tantamount to tying him to a chair and then asking him to defend himself.

When I first went into armature and professional boxing, as a 2nd dan karataka some years ago, I did not expect to hold my own in a foreign arena. I went in as a beginner and took many beatings to learn a new art. The same when I went into wrestling, I didn't go in there as a boxing coach and a fourth dan in Karate I went in there as a novice wrestler and I got beaten more than the proverbial egg until I learned and became proficient at that art also.

The indomitable Gracies in America have gone some way to redress the balance by creating the UFC (Ultimate Fight Competition) in America where any combatant of any weight and from any system can enter.

The restrictions are few and reality hits you like a hammer in the eye in this arena. It has been proven over and again, the grappler seems to prevail and succeed against all other systems.

The critics have been quick to say how scruffy and aesthetic displeasing the UFC is (like or loath the UFC it does make its point rather well) because, they claim, the kickers and punchers have not been of a high enough standard. Welcome to the real world lads. Scruffy is where it's at when the pavement is your arena. The reason the UFC is so scruffy is not because of the poor standard of the vertical fighters - some of them are world class in their own arts - rather it is because 'that's reality', in a real fight scruffy is exactly how it gets.

But twenty years of crisp martial art, of compliance and of celluloid pier pressure has indoctrinated many contemporary fighters with the belief that 'if it don't look nice it's no good'.

One of the main reasons why Judo has become, predominantly, a standing art is because ground fighting is not pleasing to the untrained eye, and this is also the reason why the devastating art of amateur wrestling, once pre-dominantly a ground fighting art also, is now such a minority sport. It is also the main reason behind the decline, nay death, of the 'real' wrestling and wrestlers of the late nineteenth to early twentieth century. Legendary fighters like Stanislous Zabisco, George Hackenschmidt, Bert Asarati, Karl Pojello etc are never heard of any more. People did not (even though they said they did) want reality they wanted flash, they did not want three second encounters they wanted epic battles, they did not want opponents being mauled to the ground they wanted them balletically thrown with a spectacular suplex. It was a paradox:

the spectator wanted epic battles and panache, and they got it in the end, but insisted that the fights be real and were absolutely appalled when the wrestlers turned to 'show', to give them what they wanted. So now we have ended up with spectacular, but totally unreal, bouts of wrestling, and not because the fighters cannot fight for real rather because the audience does not want real - even if they say they do.

The great Jack Sherry of Alaska, world wrestling champion in the early 1900s, would defeat opponents so quickly that spectators would often still be coming into the stadium when the fight was already over - Jack was a promoter's nightmare but he absolutely refused to 'show' to please the crowd. Sherry never lost a fall and toured the world offering 10,000 dollars to anyone who could pin him or any boxer who could stand up to him (with no holds barred) for 90 seconds. No one ever collected the 10,000 dollars.

Eventually, due mostly to public demand and strong willed promoters, wrestlers were forced to 'show'. It was then that wrestling started to fall into decline, which was a crying shame because the wrestlers of old were marvellous athletes capable of some amazing displays of strength and stamina. Bert Asarati - one of my personal favourites - fought in over 7000 fights around the world, losing only a handful, and finished his working life as a kind of mobile club minder. Whenever there was trouble at a local club the patrons would call for Mr Asarati, who would arrive in a limo. Five foot six tall, weighing 17 stone, he took up two seats on a train yet at the age of 45 he could still hold a one armed hand stand for 45 seconds. He single-handedly calmed any trouble. Often just his presence alone was enough. On one occasion he was called to a huge riot at a club, and when he arrived the patron was astounded, 'But we have a riot' he said 'and you have come on your own'. Mr Asarati looked at the battling crowds and then back to the patron and said very calmly 'One man one riot'. He then quickly dispelled the fighting crowds - most ran just at the sight of him.

In the martial arts we have, to a degree, suffered the same fate. Everyone has become so obsessed about getting Olympic recognition that their arts have become watered down and aesthetic, the 'blood and snot' elements of martial that disqualified them as spectator sports were removed to make them more pleasing to the spectator. Many of our combatants have become brilliant athletes but our art is a poor and diluted facsimile of its former self. Many arts have become neutered, their potency surgically removed by the keen blade of the political briefcase martial artist that sits at every association meeting scoring ippons and wazaris over his fellow members with verbatim quotations of association rules, paragraphs and sub paragraphs. The same ilk that killed wrestling to make it more commercial are 'corpsing up' the martial arts.

I have no argument with sport or the Olympics or anything else for that matter but let's keep it in context: martial art is not sport - although the sport element is a good by-product. It is not 'show', though show is a nice was to 'peddle our wares' - it is many things not least a method of self defence.

Many of the modern martial artists have lost sight of their original aim. Extinction is biting at our heels and, if we are not careful, we will suffer the fate of those before us.

Stripped of reality many of the arts have become emaciated aerobic routines that entertain on the stage but do not function in the arena. Subsequently, when placed under the pressure of reality, they crumble. The UFC has already shown some elements of this to all but the blind.

However, as big a fan as I am of the UFC, it is still different from defence in the street for many reasons.

Three Second Fighter

Street defence is not match fighting - that noble art died with my father's generation. Rather it is, mostly, a three second affair where the leading technique is dialogue and deception and, more often than not, one blow - usually a punch - decides the outcome. This is what I call the 'sniper option', or what the original 'men' of martial art would have called the one punch kill.

That is the ethos of 'The Three Second Fighter', forming a game plan, perfecting one or two short range techniques as a main artillery, using awareness of our surroundings and of the enemy as our bedrock, deception as our primer, distraction as our trigger and sniper option to eclipse the enemy.

This book is not meant to be disrespectful to any martial art or artists. I am a big fan of all the arts and have many friends in many systems. So, if offence is taken then you have my unreserved apologies before we start: my aim is to educate not exasperate.

Chapter One
Changing times

I am aware that the times are changing, but so many people, it would seem, are not. The reason I am aware is because I am still out there and can see just how badly prepared many people are for the realities of street combat. They don't have a game plan, a main artillery (what's that?) or a support system. All they have, no offence intended, is an antiquated art and a false sense of security. They say that change is sacrilege - I say that change is sense if survival is your pre-requisite.

Some claim that they have no interest in self protection/ adaptation etc. If that is the case and you are training art for art's sake - an admirable goal let me add - the workability of art will be off no concern to you and to read on will be a waste of your time.

Others claim to have long since transcended such trivia and now train art for art's sake and practice technique for technique's sake, yet when you ask them about the modern enemy, about game plans, about empirical knowledge they haven't got a clue. They have no reference points and cannot meet the question with an articulate answer, so, in a way, they have transcended embryonically. You cannot rise above the physical elements of martial until you have first met and overcome them - like trying to take an advanced driving test before you have learned how to drive. Many people use transcendency and 'art' as a hiding place because reality scares the pants off them and they don't have an answer. Some of them would like to find an answer but their ego will not allow them to climb down from their high, often self erected, pedestal and become a beginner again in order to acquire the knowledge. Deep down they know that they are travelling down the wrong path but bury that knowledge deep into the sub-conscious. Others still see a glimpse of the truth in an article/book/video or on a seminar but are simply not strong enough to accept it because to admit may mean to change direction and after going the wrong way for so many years they can't bear the thought of having to go all the way back and start again.

As Sir Winston Churchill said 'Many men stumble upon the truth then get back up and walk off as though nothing happened'.

This is not to say that these people are not working hard hacking away to make a path through their metaphoric jungle, rather it is to say that they are simply hacking in the wrong jungle.

Others still, put up a fence to hide their inadequacies by trying to ridicule the messenger saying that it is he who has lost his 'way' and not them.

A friend once tried this tired routine on me. He hinted that I'd lost my 'way' because I left traditional Karate as a second dan and that my grades since then, even though they were all bona fide and with a governing body, were not 'real' grades. He felt that because I left Karate and found my own direction I had sold out - lost my way and now taught a diluted art. Basically, I have many grades in many systems but they mean very little to me. I haven't worn a black belt for many years and whilst it is nice to hold the grades I will not use them as a crutch to support an ailing mentality, neither do I condemn others for staying with tradition and with the grading syllabus - I think it is a fine idea.

I never lost my way, I just found a better way for me and was strong enough to change direction even though I knew I'd be seen by many as a maverick.

You don't have to change arts to meet the modern enemy, you only have to change conceptions and update so that it fits in with the present environment and adapt to the aggressor of today.

The power base of all arts should be that its exponents develop enlightenment and become better people, that they temper ferocious fighting ability with kindness and compassion and that they learn to control their negative emotions like greed, envy, jealousy, ego etc. Ultimately their integrity should be without question. Enlightenment should allow them to have a full perspective of their own weaknesses and strengths both physically and mentally (how many times have you heard an instructor say 'we don't need to grapple in our art because we are too good to be taken to ground' or 'our art is too dangerous to pressure test' etc?). It should also allow them a paradoxical understanding of other systems and that theirs is not the only way. The true warrior, the one who has nothing to prove to himself and no ego to defend, will be able to walk away from a potentially confrontational situation.

And yet we look around us at our seniors, the ones that we wish to emulate, and they often display all the bad characteristics that you might expect of a lower graded person. Many are not honest, they cheat on their partners, they are egotists - they refuse to let their students train in other systems or with other instructors, they are envious when others around them, even their own students, succeed when instead they should be pleased. Many are greedy, ungrateful, discourteous even bullying.

When I teach an art I try to teach my students to be nice people. If they find themselves confronted by a potentially threatening situation I teach them first to avoid, second to escape, third to use dissuasive verbal and, as a last resort, to be as ferocious as the situation demands. In the present climate that is very ferocious indeed.

This is not to decry all martial artists: I have met many people who are excellent role models and who have truly found their way, people I look up to; sadly I have also met many who have drifted to the dark side

Three Second Fighter

To the people that read my books, those perceptive enough to be searching for the grail of martial, I think is important that you know where I'm coming from. I'm not frightened to tell you how it is out there (in your face) but I'm not frightened to tell you either that violence should be a last resort. That's not to say that you let your aggressor attack first. If you can't walk away from a situation you should, out of necessity, be pre-emptive - rather it is to say that if there is a more affable solution to a smack in the eye, use it.

I've digressed a little, par for the course with me. Changing times means updating our arts. In every other aspect of society things around us update to keep in line with evolution: cars change every year, computers seem to change and update every other minute, modern warfare/weapons etc are constantly under review. And yet in the martial arts we are still practising concepts, in the hope that they will enable us to better defend ourselves in what is fast becoming a sticky world, that were better designed to fight samurai on horseback. Amazingly, and this kind of logic absolutely astounds me. People say, 'well - it's been around for thousands of years and it worked for our forefathers so there must be something in it'! A horse and cart worked for our forefathers, but that doesn't mean that we should give up the 2.5 injection.

Again, this does not mean abandoning arts that have taken thousands of years to develop, rather it means altering or tailoring them to fit the new environment - the modern enemy. We are no longer fighting a long range enemy at a pre-arranged time on a battlefield. We are no longer facing brave warriors with budo as their way. We are facing a cowardly enemy, a deceptive enemy, a short range enemy and our time of battle is not pre-arranged, we are rarely forewarned of an imminent attack, there will be no warm up, no formal bow, no slap of hand or touch of glove - most people are taken out of the game before they even realise that they are in it. Do you really think that if the founders of these systems were around today that they'd still be working with their original technique and concepts? Not a chance. They'd have updated in a hurry, let me tell you.

This suite of clothes that we call martial art is ill-fitting for the 21st century, but that does not mean that we must discard it, rather we should re-tailor it so that it does fit. Let's toss the horse and cart into the museums and get us a vehicle that will stand the fast pace of contemporary violence - or fall victim to the onslaught of the modern aggressor. You do not have to throw away tradition/ kata/forms/etiquette etc. because there will always be a place for these worthy attributes - if you go down and train with Gary Spiers, the godfather of applied karate, you will see him still teaching the karate rudiments. But he teaches them with a realistic bent.

Chapter Two
Awareness - the power base

'Whilst it is true that prevention is better than cure one still has to address the physical response necessary when a situation becomes live. In many quarters its tuition is and has been grossly misrepresented by the 'physical response syndrome'. This misrepresentation is often being taught by people whose only experience of violent conflict has patently been in the arena of their own safe imagination where hypothesis wins the day. They write, evidently, from a perspective of never having been there themselves and garnish unreal scenarios with unworkable physical techniques.'
Peter Consterdine - British Combat Association

Most people are not mentally or physically equipped to handle a violent confrontation. The immediate response for the majority being that of terror and capitulation. For this reason self protection should deal with the possibility of 'flight' over 'fight'. Where flight is not an option, awareness of attack ritual should be used by the potential victim to prime and pre-emptively attack the attacker.

If you have to become physical you should be pre-emptive and not defensive. Of course, once you have been attacked pre-emptiveness is no longer an option and most of the techniques that are the perfunctory by-products of most defence books are as unworkable as they are unrealistic. If you are not already incapacitated you will be fighting, tooth and nail, for your life. This is where the support system, to be detailed in a later chapter, comes into its own.

Awareness allows a pre-emptive response, (avoidance, escape or attack) the victim recognising menace before the 'monster metamorphosis', this allowing him/her to deal with it before it deals with them.

The majority of contemporary street encounters are not blind side ambushes - though these still have to be addressed - neither are they match fights - though these have to be taken into account also - rather they are attacks preceded by ritualistic, though often innate, priming entrapments.

Everyone, it would appear, addresses the physical response - and each school of thought, of which there are many, seems to contradict the other - but what about those vital seconds before combat, pre-fight ritual, the build up that often dictates the outcome of the fight? Though often subconsciously the attacker uses priming techniques that allow him to take his intended victim out of the game before they even know that they are in it, recognising these ritualistic movements allows you to read the attacker's play - control him and, if he persists in his attempted assault, take him off the planet. There is an old proverb that says if you want to go in to the woods and hunt the tiger you first must learn everything there is to know about the tiger, his weaknesses and his strengths, his pre-attack body language, where he sleeps, eats, his likes and dislikes, his reactions to certain stimuli. You need to know your enemy inside out - otherwise you are not hunting the tiger, you are simply taking a walk in the woods.

What do you know about the enemy?

Knowledge is power - to make our techniques work against today's enemy we need empirical background on him, we need to study his weaknesses and strengths, his rituals - the body language and street speak he uses prior to attack. If you don't understand the enemy then you are fighting blindfold.

Three Second Fighter

If you talk to a game hunter he will be able to tell you what every movement of his prey means and how the animal is likely to react to different stimuli, he will also tell you the exact movements his prey will make before it attacks, this being exactly the right to shoot. The game hunter knows his enemy as well as he knows himself and it is not the weapon he carries in his hand that makes him superior rather his vast knowledge of the animal's attack ritual.

A nightclub doorman, a good one, is a master of body language and enemy ritual. He can spot a fight seconds, minutes even hours before it starts simply by studying the customers in his club.

The monster walking back and forward on the edge of the dance floor, stalking his intended prey (the guy dancing with his girlfriend, the lad who accidentally bumped into him and spilled his drink, etc), his back heaving as he breathes deeply to control adrenalin, his arms splaying as though he's carrying buckets of water, tunnel vision - he doesn't take his eye off his prey - the verbal abuse 'wanker, wanker, arsehole'.

He is building up to an attack, but when he reaches the crescendo and is just about to strike - that's when he is most vulnerable to attack himself.

Sun Tzu said it far more eloquently that I ever could:

"Know the enemy and know yourself;
One hundred challenges without danger;
Know the enemy and know not yourself;
One triumph for one defeat;
Know not the enemy and know not yourself'
Every challenge is certain peril."

The ritual of violence

Most attacks are preceded by stalking and dialogue entrapments.

One area often overlooked is the innate ritual employed by attackers. One aspect of this being the four D's - dialogue-deception-distraction-destruction - this involving body language as well as the spoken word. This dialogue is often called 'The interview'.

If you can spot the ritual, you can stop the crime.

Street speak

The language of the street also needs deciphering, much of the attacker's dialogue is used as an innate trigger for violence. Positive interpretation will unveil signs of imminent attack.

The ritual alters according to the category of attack, as does the dialogue. The genre of attack can vary from gratuitous assault to serial rape/murder.

If the intent is robbery or rape or the attacker is a seasoned one, the dialogue is usually disarming or incidental, 'Have you got a light please?' Or 'Haven't we met somewhere before?' The attacker looking to 'switch the victim off' before attack.

In the case of the gratuitous assault where the intent is 'attack for attack's sake' the dialogue will probably be aggressive, 'What are you looking at?' In either case, dialogue is employed to gain and distract attention before attack.

Generally speaking, the greater the crime, the greater the deception.

At the bottom end of the scale the gratuitous attacker will engage his intended victim with aggressive dialogue, ('I'm gonna batter you, you bastard!'). At the top of the scale the rapist/murderer will prime his victim with anything from a gentlemanly request for directions to, as in the case of killer John Cannan, sending his intended victims (usually women he had spotted in the street and followed, or just met) champagne, flowers and a dinner invitation, that were the ultimate primers for rape and murder. The elite attackers dropping in to the thespian role with Oscar winning perfection.

The street fighter

In the case of an experienced street fighter he will often tell his intended victim that he does not want to fight - then attack them immediately and ferociously, usually finishing the fight with the same attack. If he says that he does not want to fight and then moves away he is probably telling the truth and is not such a threat. If, however, he moves forward and tries to make body contact as he tells you 'I don't want any trouble!' then he is usually a liar and is using the deception to prime you for attack.

I have a friend in Coventry, who shall remain nameless, who always told his opponents that he did not want to fight before knocking them out. Invariably they would come around, some moments later, rubbing their chin and saying 'I'm sure he said he didn't want to fight!'

Cheap shot? Dirty trick? Cowardly move? No, not at all and if you think it is any, or all three, of the former then wake up and smell the roses. I understand where you're coming from, I used to be the same, with the enemy of this generation. Forget it - he is brutal and shameless and to give him honour when he will only use it against you is fool hardy. You need an edge, you may be facing two or three and if they beat you it will be brutal - you can't afford to lose - so use what ever you can to survive the encounter. And if you think that it is below you then look at the Samurai of old: they used many such tricks and mass deception to defeat a dangerous enemy, everything from feigning cowardice, pre-fight, to disarm an enemy before attacking themselves, to feigning injury, in-fight, to draw an opponent in for the kill and thus generate an opening in his defence, to brutally hacking him to pieces, post fight, as a propaganda exercise to frighten off other potential enemies. Morality in real violence will do nothing but blunt your tools, so reserve this very worthy attribute for those in society, and in your own life, that deserve it.

Gratuitous assault

This mindless fashion of violence often starts with as little as eye contact; this in a volatile habitat being construed as a subliminal 'challenge to fight'. Many of the fights I witnessed in my time as a nightclub doorman began with the 'eye contact challenge'.

You don't have to do anything wrong to be attacked by the by people of this ilk, you just have to be there. Being aware of surroundings and attack ritual will allow you to detect and subsequently avoid these incidents in the primary stages.

In the bar or on the street you can easily spot the gratuitous attacker. He'll have a bad attitude, probably propping up the bar or stalking the dance floor, his elbows pushed out from his sides as though carrying buckets of water. He'll have the customary curled upper lip and will probably be very rude to anyone that moves within a few feet of him. If he's walking down the street he'll do so with an over confident/arrogant bounce, if he's with others he'll probably be very loud, garrulous and erratic in his movements. Again, as in the night club, he'll be stalking, looking for eye contact. If you are aware you can spot these signs a mile off. There are two kinds of eye contact that may escalate in to violence.

The cursory glance

Who accidentally catches your eye, or you his, the glance becoming a stare, and progressing to a verbal exchange, this the pre-cursor to violence.

Often, when it becomes obvious that you do not know each other, the ego clicks in and goes to work. The initial cursory eye contact develops into a fully fledged staring contest. The eyes, being a sensitive organ, cannot hold a stare for too long without the occurrence of soreness, watering or blinking. Not wanting to blink first, this possibly being construed as a 'back down', the one with the sorest eyes throws a verbal challenge ('You ****ing looking at me?') to hide the fact that he needs to blink. If the verbal challenge is returned ('Yea, I am looking at you. What you gonna do about it?') then the fight, after a few more formalities, is probably on.

'The eye contact challenger'

This is the man who is looking for a fight, the first person to hold eye contact with him will become his victim, his aggression is usually displaced but, nevertheless, tangibly ferocious.

These are his ritualistic steps
1)   EYE CONTACT
You may catch the eye of someone across a crowded room or a street, the look lingers.

2)   THE QUESTION
"Who are you looking at? Want a ****ing picture?"

3)   THE APPROACH
A physical approach follows.

4)   QUESTION REITERATION
"I said, do you want a ****ING picture?" The reiteration, with added vehemence.

5)   ACTUAL CHALLENGE
"Do you wanna 'go', then?"

6)   SINGLE SYLLABLE CHALLENGE

Often the assailant may attack at 'actual challenge'. If he doesn't, and as a pre-cursor to violence, he will often drop in to single syllables that act as subliminal action triggers to his attack. Words like 'Yeah', 'And' or 'So', are often employed just before attack. The single syllable is a sure sign that the interview is nearing an end and the introduction of physical is imminent.

Running concurrently will be signs of 'adrenal reaction', displayed by the challenger.

Arm splaying

The attacker's arms will splay in a fit of exclamation.

The finger's come-on

He will often beckon his victim on with his finger.

Head nodding

The assailant may sporadically nod his head.

Neck Pecking

He will peck his neck like a cockerel usually in conjunction with his single syllable challenge.

Eye bulge

Due to the tunnel vision that accompanies adrenalin the attacker's eyes may appear wide and staring.

Stancing up

He will take up an innate fighting stance.

Distance close-down

With every passing second of the altercation the attacker will advance closer to his victim, his movements and tone becoming more erratic and aggressive the closer he gets to actual attack.

It is worth mentioning that the forgoing is the complete ritual. Occasionally, depending upon the victim's response and awareness and the attacker's temperament, the attacker may attack without warning at any stage or jump steps, for instance from the question to the actual challenge, so an early exit is always advisable.

The earlier you can spot the ritual the more chance you have of being pre-emptive in avoidance escape or attack.

Ideally you should avoid eye contact, or break it if it is already engaged, as soon as you sense menace. If a verbal challenge is made, do not return it - the verbal will be thrown as a subliminal challenge and a reply will usually be seen as an acceptance of that challenge. If an approach is made put up your fence (detailed later).

The disarming approach
The mugger/rapist/seasoned fighter

The professional attacks for profit and covets compliance. He does not want to fight. To make his job easier he employs guile as opposed to force, this coming via deception. As with all predators, he seeks people in a victim state. He is, most often, very different from the archetypal, celluloid attacker that we have been programmed to expect.

I think this is best described By Christopher Berry-Dee and Robin Odell in their true crime book 'Lady Killer'. I quote,

"Such predators are difficult to detect because their behaviour is masked with protective cunning. They merge into society and appear to all intents and purposes normal and well adjusted."

This is the case with the most disarming of predators. They rarely look like potential attackers. The archetypal stocking faced robber with a cosh and a swag bag is far removed from the real world villain who is more likely to be dressed in a Boss smart suit and an Italian tie.

The opportunities they seek are those formerly described. Often the attacker may not even be looking, but if an opportunity falls into their lap, they will act.

Again, intentions vary. The muggers I have interviewed intended to rob, the rapists intended to rape, often killing their victims as an afterthought, or by mistake. The killers sometimes intended to kill, other times they too killed by accident. The more serious the crime and experienced the criminal the more deceptive the priming, the attackers adopting a cunning veil to beguile their intended victims.

I shall deal with them individually, still bearing in mind that they all use deception in varying degrees.

Note: If you do not employ awareness, deception often becomes an unnecessary tool for the attacker, the 'blind side/ambush attack' prevailing. In this instance the first the victim knows of the incursion is the physical attack itself, by then it is often too late.

As with most attacks the mugger follows a ritual. Understanding this is the pre-requisite to threat avoidance.

The Mugger

"There was this geezer and his Mrs, outside a telephone box. Their car had the bonnet up, the woman went in to the phone box. We walked up to the phone box and pretended to queue for the phone. The geezer looked like he had money, good clothes, smart car. I gave J. the signal by winking at him, I then asked the geezer the time and we both pulled out our knives. When he looked up we told him to hand over his wallet."

Mugger interview

These are his ritualistic steps.

1) VICTIM SELECTION

"Choosing a victim isn't hard. People are just asking to be robbed. I came out of Pizza Hut the other night, about 10.30pm, there was this girl walking down the side of the dual carriageway, on her own. She must have only been, what, 17, at the very most. She might as well have had a sign across her chest saying, 'attack me!' Then they moan when someone does attack them. And the lads are as bad. They haven't got a ****ing clue. We used to thumb a lift from town, after the nightclub. Some ****ing idiot would pick us up, three of us, then wonder what he'd done wrong when we mugged 'im for all 'e's got. I reckon 'alf the ****ers aren't all there. I mean, don't they read the papers? Don't they know 'ow we (muggers) work?"

Case histories

The ideal victim is in code white (switched off), mentally and/or environmentally, those daydreaming or detached from the herd.

Selection often occurs in sparsely populated locations, the mugger wanting as little fuss as possible in the execution of his attack. He favours the quiet park/street/entry etc. This does not mean that people are safe in highly populated areas like shopping malls, busy streets etc. Very often the mugger stalks such places for victims, after selection following them to a safe attack zone like the car park of a mall.

There are of course different kinds of mugger. Some will see an opportunity and snatch and run, others will stalk and prime, others still are opportunists who will only attack if a safe opportunity falls into their lap. Awareness will allow you to spot these malevolents and avoid attack.

2) VICTIM STALKING

"Once we've chosen a victim we follow them, cross the road, walk past them maybe two or three times. We wait for them to walk into a side street or park, anywhere quiet. Some of them must be thick not to notice what's going on."

Case histories

A stalking of the chosen victim, for priming, and awareness assessment, will occur. If necessary the victim will be followed in the hope that he/she will heighten vulnerability mentally/ environmentally by walking into a park/down a quiet street/entry etc. If the victim is followed from a shopping mall the attacker often waits for him/her to put the shopping in the boot of the car or even strike as he/she enters the car. It is at such times that even vigilant people drop their guard, and though it may only be for a second that is all the attacker needs.

3) EXPLORATORY APPROACH

"We walk up to them and ask the time, this distracts them. If they look like they know what we're gonna do, or if they look a bit tough or answer with a rough voice, when we ask them the time, then we just walk off.

Case histories

This will often be coupled with disarming dialogue, (the four D's) used to prime the victim for attack. It is also used as a secondary awareness assessment.

If at this point, or at any point after victim stalking, the victim appears switched off, the mugger may initiate his attack/threatened attack with out any further priming.

4) ASSESSMENT
a) NEGATIVE ASSESSMENT
If the mugger feels that the chosen victim is switched on to the attempt and his secondary assessment is negative, he will often abort.

b) POSITIVE ASSESSMENT
"...this distracts them (asking the time) while we pull out our knives. When they look up we say, 'Give us your ****ing money!' They usually look blank. Both of us shout at them, 'Get your ****ing wallet out', and put the knives closer to their face."

Case histories

If the mugger feels that the chosen victim is switched off he may initiate the attack/threatened attack whilst the victim is engaged in answering his disarming question (this may be anything from asking directions to asking the time).

5) THREATENED ATTACK
"...This was taking too long (the mugging) I thought to myself. I said, 'I'm going to give you to the count of three [to hand over his wallet], or else', and pushed the knife closer to his throat. He handed over his wallet and we ran off. If he'd refused to give us the wallet by three, we'd have just run away."

Case histories

The mugger will often threaten the victims with attack to frighten them into supplication, frequently underlining the threat with a weapon or an accomplice, or both.

32

The threat will be aggressive and menacing, this effecting adrenal dump in the victim, quickly escalating to the freeze syndrome (the reasoning process mistakes adrenalin for fear, often freezing victims into immobility). The threats are repeated with escalating aggression causing the victim to experience multiple adrenal release, grossly heightening the supposed feeling of fear and adding to the 'freeze'. The threats of course are married with demands for money/credit cards etc.

The false promise

Often the mugger threatens to hurt the victim if they are not compliant, or *not* to hurt the victim in exchange for compliance. The promise cannot be relied on.

6) ACTUAL ATTACK

"Sometimes, if they're a bit brave I'll give them a dig, (hit them) then they're mine. I've 'ad blokes who really look like they're gonna go for it, you give them a bit of pain and the fight falls out of them. They become just like babies."

Case histories

The mugger may use a physical attack, creating compliance via disablement.

Some muggers will initiate an attack to disable the victim, before stealing his/her belongings.

Sometimes the attack will be minimal, used only to add to 'freeze', other times the attack will be frenzied and severe. Any chance of a physical defence, other than actually attacking back with the same degree (or greater) of ferocity, is unlikely to be effective. The concepts of 'blocking' an assailant's blows or using hypothesised 'release' techniques are not sound. If the situation has got this far only the very strong will survive.

Body language

Most attackers will display the following body language in the course of their ritual.

1) Erratic eye movement

The attacker or his accomplice, concerned about being caught mid act, will constantly be checking for police/general public involvement.

2) Adrenal reaction

Unless the attacker is seasoned he will be showing signs of adrenalin. Pre-attack, his face will appear pale, his eyes wide from adrenalin-induced tunnel vision. He will be stern and unsmiling, he may also fidget in an attempt to hide 'adrenal shake' (the body will 'shiver' as though cold) and his voice may have a nervous quiver.

3) Hand concealment

Pre-attack, if the attacker is carrying a weapon, the bearing hand may be hidden, either in his pocket or behind his back. If one or both of his hands is concealed, beware. Some attackers do not hide the hands, rather they turn the palm or palms away from the chosen victim on approach to conceal a weapon, or keep the offending hand close to their leg to conceal the same. Other attackers will keep their hands on full display, extracting a weapon from its hiding place as they approach, or immediately after asking an engaging question.

If the approach is by more than one person they will all usually display the same physical traits.

Pincer movement

If more than one assailant is involved it is usual for one of the attackers to deploy the victim with a distracting question whilst the other/s move to your off side, whilst the victim is distracted by the questioner, his accomplice/s attack.

Tell-tale signs

Awareness allows you to spot the tell-tale signs that the mugger emits in his selection stage.

Close observation will highlight the assailant's suspicious actions, he will stand out like a sore thumb. His eyes will follow the victim closely and dart away if the look is returned, he will have a false casualness about him, as though trying to look occupied, but with no occupying matter. The fact that he has noticed his intended victim's vigilance will, at this stage, usually be enough to cause early abortion of the intended attack. Awareness deems the victim a hard target. The victim should let the attacker know, by his/her actions, that he has been noted. If the victim mingles with other people, goes in to a shop, makes a hasty retreat etc. the attacker will move on, going back into selection mode and looking for another victim, preferably someone that is not so aware.

So remember, the attacker is not a compliant training partner in the dojo who will go with the flow; your attacker will be aggressive, uncompliant and ***ing frightening. But this hard shell usually conceals a coward, and once you have cracked the shell and got past his front the attacker usually goes from 'hard to lard'.

Chapter Three
Muscle memory

Did you ever hear the story about the circus knife thrower that tried to kill his wife but every tine he threw a knife at her he missed? He had trained so hard and for so long to just miss her that when he actually wanted to hit her he couldn't - his muscle memory was tuned into missing the target.

I was sat at the Shotokan Midlands championships a few years ago watching fine displays of competition fighting by some of the top point scorers in the country. One of the fighters, G, a member of the then Midland squad and an excellent competition fighter with some twenty years karate experience behind him (he was a 3rd dan at the time) approached me in the stands. He looked rather perturbed and asked whether I could give him a little advice.

It turned out that this guy had, several weeks before, been involved in a fracas outside a local night club. He'd had a good night out with his brother and a friend and had just left the club to get some chips, as you do, and make his way home. Crossing the road he caught the eye of two aggressive young lads on the other side of the street. Both were about twenty years old.

'What are you ****ing looking at?' the lad shouted across to G.

Because the question was unsolicited and completely unexpected G didn't really know what to say, so he hesitated. Before he knew it the lad had crossed the road with his mate and was reiterating the challenge,

'D'you ****ing want some then, do ya, ****ing do ya?'

His brother and his mate tried to pull G away telling him not to get involved and that it wasn't worth it. G still had not spoken because he just didn't know how to reply. Basically he was gobsmacked, the challenge had come completely out of the blue.

As he said to me in the stands, 'If I'd had trouble with the guy earlier on I'd have known what to expect, but I hadn't, this guy wanted to fight with me for no reason. I just couldn't understand it.'

Unfortunately this is the way with many attacks today. G was searching for logic - there was none.

The lad got more and more aggressive, his mate hovered menacingly in the background as back up, until he was almost in G's face. Instinctively G threw a punch at the guy, pre-emptively, and landed what would have been a perfect knock-out blow on his aggressor's jaw had he not pulled the punch on impact with perfect competition winning control. His brother pulled him away and again told him to 'leave it'.

As they turned to walk away G felt a heavy blow to the back of his head followed by a few more. His brother and their mate suffered the same fate - within seconds all three had been beaten to the floor and given a good kicking whilst down.

G never slept for a week and, as he spoke to me, several weeks after the incident it was obvious that he was still beating himself up over the matter.

Why hadn't he performed? Why did he pull his punch? Why was he so scared? He'd spent all his adult life and much of his young life training in a fighting art and on his first real encounter it had let him down.

The bumps and bruises didn't bother him that much, it was the fact that he felt so ineffectual in the encounter that really stung, and their attackers were nobodies - hadn't trained a day in their lives. G seemed to me as though he was on the verge of abandoning his art because of the debacle.

What went wrong? What should he do?

Firstly I told him not to abandon his art. The art he practised, Shotokan, was a good art - a hard style. What he did need to do was change the way he trained.

You get what you train for. If you train for control and practice thousands of pulled punches day in and day out then when you are attacked and spontaneity takes the reins in a real fight, pulled punches are what you'll most likely get. It's called muscle memory. When you repetitively train a technique it will become a reaction, what we call automatism. You will automatically do what your body is trained to do, and if that training is to pull punches on impact with the target then that's what you'll do in a real situation.

I remember many years ago at a big international semi-contact in France meeting when things got out of hand and tempers started to fray, the whole contest arena exploded and everyone started fighting for real - and there was some of the best fighters on the planet at this contest - but, amazingly, not a single injury was incurred. This was not because the fighters were incapable - they were brilliant - it was because muscle memory pumped out what they had all trained so diligently for, they had trained to pull blows and that's exactly what they did. The guy who reported the incident in a big martial arts magazine could not understand why, considering the fact that these were the best karataka in the world, the techniques, when used for real, did not work. He put it down to the fact that 'Karate is obviously not all it is made out to be!'

In actual fact it was not karate that was ineffectual rather the training methods. These guys, like the circus knife thrower, were trained to miss and not hit, and that's exactly what they did.

Muscle memory is a good thing if you train it correctly. If you want it to feed out full contact blows in a real scenario then full contact blows is what you must train for. This is one of the reasons why training in semi-contact and full contact at the same time is not always a good thing. The first punch I ever threw on the door was pulled on impact and did nothing but cut my opponent's lip. I thought it was because I didn't have any power in my technique, but when I realised that it was negative muscle memory I changed all my training to full contact. Subsequently I was knocking people out in real fights but getting disqualified from every tournament I entered. People thought that I was dropping my contest opponents deliberately, but I wasn't, it was muscle memory.

Muscle memory also affects your reactions to capitulation. If you stop in the dojo when you get a bloody lip or when you're tired or nauseous or scared, if you give in too easily in the controlled arena that's exactly what you should expect to do in a real situation. So in the controlled arena you must treat it as though it were for real. If you stop in a real fight because of a misdemeanour then you'll be waking up with a crowd around you - of this there is no doubt.

Muscle memory can be over-ridden in certain circumstances. When you use a sniper option, which is response as opposed to reaction, you can actually monitor the amount of control (or lack thereof) that you wish to use but, once that first shot has been taken and spontaneity takes over, muscle memory is the order of the day.

If you do mix your training, a bit of semi and a bit of full, muscle memory tends to go with the majority, that is it will favour whichever you train the most.

If it is reality that you favour, and I presume that it is otherwise you would not be reading this book, then stick to as much full contact, pad work, bag work, heavy sparring etc, as you can.

Compliance

In many of the systems around today compliance rules the roost. This is a bad thing for several reasons.

Compliance is good when you are learning a new technique. If there is not a bit of compliance on the side of your partner it becomes very difficult to improve, but it should be used as little as possible and not all the time. Otherwise you will build a false sense of security and confidence that will get you bashed in a real situation.

Use compliance to develop good technique and then throw it away and practice without it, especially in grappling work. Whilst a compliant partner helps you to develop technique, an un-compliant partner will help you develop manipulative strength, stamina, endurance, true confidence and an enlightenment of what works and what does not. The latter is something that cannot be found without pressure testing one's wares. When you make a technique work against someone that is wholly determined to stop you then you know that technique is of some worth.

I guarantee that if a war started tomorrow and martial artists from different systems had to make their art work in life and death situations all the shit would drop, no one would be practising superfluous technique and everyone would be looking to reinstate the illegal techniques (the ones that really did and do work) that have long since been exiled from contemporary martial art because they were not commercially/socially/Olympically acceptable in a civilised?! society. When you know that it has got to work or you die you don't **ck about trying to make it look good. And you certainly wouldn't be practising decidedly 'iffy' technique. You'd end up, like I did, with a small but proven main artillery that you are absolutely sure of, and a massive support system to back those techniques up.

Many of the wonderful systems (I shall name none because I do not wish to offend) that originated as 'real' arts have met this decline and will only realise it when they fail the acid test of workability.

So I ask you, do you pressure test? How will your system fare when the rug of compliance is pulled from under your feet?

Please don't anyone be offended by this, I mean no disrespect and if you are offended you have my unreserved apology, but if you want reality then honesty - often it is self honesty - is the first step.

This is not about style or system. I have seen none that would not work though I have seen many that are practised in a way that would make them fail.

If you are in a club where you do not feel fear and where pressure is not injected on a regular basis then maybe you should be looking to change clubs.

Another bad thing about too much compliance is that it teaches you to be beaten. You actually learn to let your opponent put a move or a technique on you, often placing yourself in the right position when he has got it wrong - in a sense you learn to lose which can't be a good thing.

I spar with my brother-in-law most days - I have done for many years. I also use him in my club to demonstrate techniques that I am teaching. He had been a compliant demo partner for so long that when we actually got the gloves on and went for it I found myself completely dominating him - he fell for every move that I tried. I realised that, because he had spent so much time being my compliant demo partner he had developed negative muscle memory and was getting beaten more than the proverbial egg. I told him what I thought and stopped using him for all the demo work - within weeks he was giving me the fight of my life (I'm not sure that I should have told him now) because he had erased and overrode his negative muscle memory.

Naked aggression

From my ten years experience of working the doors and my twenty five years in the martial arts I have noticed and noted many things. One of the most prominent and surprising is how people react when faced with naked aggression - it freaks them out. I've seen many fighters, some of them excellent people, bottle out when faced with an aggressive adversary even though aggression is often all that the assailant has, like a big gun with no bullets. It's menacing because you don't know that it has no bullets but harmless because of the same fact.

What naked aggression does to the recipient is signal to their brain extreme danger. Aggression is seen as synonymous with threat, the brain then sends a signal to the adrenal gland and fight or flight is put into operation. Because the brain senses extreme and imminent danger as opposed to anticipatory danger it activates a big release of adrenalin, adrenal dump, that hits the system at about a hundred miles an hour. To create this pool of extra blood needed to feed all the major muscles for fight or flight some blood is drawn away from all the non necessary areas (those seen as non necessary for fight or flight) of the body. One of these non necessary areas is the brain, and the lack of blood in the head is what causes tunnel vision, time distortion, memory loss and memory distortion, dry mouth etc.

The body also tries to off load any excess baggage, things that are not deemed needy for fight or flight. This is why we feel the urge to empty our bowels and bladder (some people actually do) or have the feeling of nausea. Of course in the twenty-first century it is not socially acceptable to empty one's bowels in public so we have learned to tighten the buttocks and control the urge.

To most, all of these reactions that we associate with being scared (look he scared, he's shaking like a leaf - he's shitting himself) are unfamiliar and so the reasoning process mistakes them for sheer terror. The panic acts as a negative body accelerator and we bottle out.

And this whole process was caused simply by aggressive stimuli that more often than not cannot be backed up.

Aggression therapy

As with most things the more exposure one gets to something and the more one understands about it the less frightening it becomes. So practice in the dojo shouting at each other, swearing and being extremely aggressive (be careful not to have children in the class when practising this exercise).

Even though it is in the controlled arena and only an exercise, the sub-conscious mind, working independently of the conscious mind, will still register trauma and release adrenalin. Whilst your opponent is shouting obscenities, you practice controlling the flow and the urge to panic. Basically you become, through constant exposure to aggression, desensitised to it (this is demonstrated on my DVD Three Second Fighter).

Of course aggression is a two way street and what can be used against us can be used by us against our attackers. Aggression can be used as a tool to instil the same adrenal dump in our assailants as they instil in us. They too, ignorant to their own bodily reactions, will often mistake adrenalin for fear and bottle out.

This is why the Kiaa points are in kata, so that we can practice switching aggression on and off like a tap. It needs practice: it is not easy to just let our aggression go at the drop of a hat. Most of us have been indoctrinated since childhood to suppress aggression and in the dojo naked aggression, displayed independently of technique, is seen as bad temper - bad control and subsequently bad etiquette, and swearing in the dojo - sacrilege. But this is a part of the modern attacker's armoury and should be a part of ours.

Learning to let your aggression out is also wonderfully therapeutic - a great way of burning up the un-utilised adrenalin left over from the intangible confrontations of twenty-first century situations like having to stand up to a belligerent boss, a dominant spouse or a noisy neighbour - confrontations where adrenalin is released but not utilised because neither fight or flight was/is an option.

People think nothing of going to the toilet every day to get rid of their physical waste but what about the psychological waste collated through so many intangible confrontations, that has to be de-sludged also?

Aggression therapy is an excellent way of exorcising the demons and de-sludging the psyche. With a bit of visualisation your training partner can become your ex-wife (though probably a lot better looking) who is still trying to dominate you even though you've been divorced 5 years, your bullying boss, noisy neighbour, your life, the whole world. Use them to tap your aggression and get it out, use it as a fuel, as an attacking implement, a psychological bullet. In my time I've beaten more opponents with aggression alone that I have with any physical attack.

With aggression therapy you can let the lot go. It helps you to mentally de-sludge and fine tune a brilliant psychological weapon, and it also helps your partner to learn control against naked aggression.

To reiterate, you get what you train for, so train for realism and that is what you get, train for compliance and all you will get is loss after loss. If you are comfortable change partners, clubs or even associations until you are uncomfortable. If you stay in a comfort zone for too long the peripheral shell will get so hardened that you won't be able to break free - which means you stop improving.

Chapter Four
The game plan (GP)

"The fox and the cat were standing on a hill, talking about how many ways they knew of escaping from a pack of dogs. The cat, feeling rather inadequate, said, 'I only know one way. I run up the nearest tree'. The fox gave the cat a sardonic smile and said, 'Well, actually, I know fifty different ways of escaping a pack of dogs.' As they spoke a pack of dogs appeared on the horizon and ran in the direction of the fox and the cat. The cat, utilising his only escape technique, found sanctuary up a nearby tree.

Whilst the fox was busy deciding which of the fifty escape techniques he should employ, he got eaten by the pack of dogs."

Some of the techniques and methods of practice in this chapter on main artillery may seem a little basic for the advanced or practising martial artist who might see 'complex' as being synonymous with effective. In real terms 'complex' is synonymous only with impractical. To be effective the chosen GP for a self defence technique must be economical and what is economical if it is not 'basic'? Paradoxically, the beginner will find no problem in practising the prescribed concepts because of their fundamental qualities and the fact that they have not been indoctrinated with negative concepts. Their cup is empty, as the Buddhist monks might say.

Game plan

> *"Thus, those that win one hundred triumphs in one hundred conflicts*
> *Do not have supreme skill.*
> *Those who have supreme skill,*
> *Use strategy (game plan) to bend others without coming to conflict.*
> *The ideal strategy, therefore, is to thwart a plan.*
> *The next best is to thwart a negotiation.*
> *The next best is to thwart a strategy.*
> *The inferior politic is to attack a fortified area.*
> *Attacking a fortified area is an art of last resort;*
> *Those skilled in executing a strategy,*
> *Bend the strategy of others without conflict;*
> *Uproot the fortifications of others with out attacking;*
> *Absorb the organisations of others without prolonged operations.*
> **Sun Tzu**

The trained fighter

We have a paradox here. In the main, the trained fighter has a huge catalogue of techniques and yet no main artillery, no support system (their whole artillery is at the range that their style dictates and very few styles adequately cover all ranges) and no game plan. He has too many techniques to chose from. When a situation becomes 'live', like the fox, he gets a mental log jam and is often defeated whilst in the process of choosing the right technique to employ.

On the other hand, the novice has 'no artillery', no game plan and absolutely no idea. When a situation becomes 'live' for him he has nothing to choose from and very often comes out of the altercation badly.

One of the philosophies of the famous Gracie family is that it is better to be excellent at one or two techniques than average at many. Rickson Gracie (pronounced Hickson) the world - no holds barred - fighting champion tells the story of a young lad who is being punched in the face by a bigger boy but is too scared to fight back. In a last ditch attempt at stopping the beating the smaller lad, by now crying, grabs hold of the bully's jacket collar with his right hand and his opposite lapel with his left and places a cross choke on the bigger boy. It's the only technique that he knows and within seconds the bully is on his knees and falling unconscious.

Unrestricted by log jam he used the only technique he knew and won a convincing victory.

Form a game plan. How will you react and what technique/s will you employ when confronted by an attacker? Decide, and then mentally and physically rehearse your game plan, over and again.

Spontaneous response

I am often told, by the uninitiated, that one should when facing an aggressor be spontaneous, reacting rather than responding according to the attack. This would mean having to wait until the assailant actually attacks, spontaneously reacting there after. Too Late!!!

Action is faster than reaction, and in the early stages of an altercation response is preferable to reaction because it allows you to control your adversary, maintain a safe range and, if necessary, utilise a sniper option. Reaction is what you get when you are ambushed or you fall in to support system because sniper option did not finish the fight, for whatever reason.

If you allow the assailant to attack first, your chances of defence are minimal.

If you are blindsided or ambushed and the first you know of a situation is the attack itself then, yes, reaction/spontaneity is not only a sound concept but the only concept you have. But, as I mentioned earlier, unless you are highly trained and pressure tested that reaction will often be a negative one and capitulation or collapse often ensues. If you wait to be attacked you have left it far too late.

If, however you are 'coded up' (using awareness) it will be pretty difficult for an assailant to utilise ambush. His attack then is likely to come from the front, and usually through deceptive dialogue. This allows you to take the initiative and determine the state of play. This is where knowledge of the enemy is imperative, his ritual and physical/verbal pre-cursors to attack allowing you to see exactly when he intends to initiate his attack and, therefore, the right time for you to escape or pre-emptively attack the attacker. His pre-cursory movements will almost give you a countdown to his physical attack.

If you do not know the modern enemy then you are only half prepared and will probably lose as often as you win. (Note: understanding yourself is comprehensively covered in my books *Animal Day* and *Fear - The friend of exceptional people*).

My advice to the novice who has no formal 'fighting' background is to choose his strongest side (right-hand if you are right-handed, left if you are left-handed) and perfect one or two techniques using that side (or whatever side you feel most confident at). Make them, via conscientious practice, your own.

Practice until you develop power and accuracy, then, especially if you employ the technique as a pre-emptive attack, your physical game plan is ready.

My advice to the advanced or practising martial artist is exactly the same: choose your strongest technique and make it stronger, work it until it is absolutely natural and comfortable. This will be your main artillery.

I remember well when Andy Sherry, a senior KUGB fighter and coach, dominated the whole European competition scene with a

Gyakasuki (reverse punch) and people were saying 'Oh yea, Andy Sherry, he's only got a reverse punch!' So what? He beat everyone in Europe with it, and in the end when his opponents looked only for this devastating reverse punch he'd slip in a big Ushuru Geri (back kick).

I have a friend in Coventry called Kev H, a phenomenal KO merchant with his right hook. He won hundreds of fights with his right hand alone, and people said to me 'Oh yea, Kev, he's only got a right hook!' Again I ask, so what? He has, to my knowledge, beaten over five hundred opponents with it. And why? Because it works and he knows it works.

When Mr Sherry fought he would, I'm sure, have used his awareness of contest arena and of the opponent in front of him to make the reverse punch fit and Kev did the same. His acute awareness meant that people found it very hard to ambush him. He was too switched on, so he made the circumstances fit his sniper option.

This of course is not to say that these two worthy fighters had nothing else other than their sniper attack. Both are/were intelligent enough to understand that a comprehensive support system was needed to back their main artillery - just in case - but they felt no obligation to change a winning formula just because the uninitiated thought that their arsenal was limited.

What this allows you to do is sit in your front room at home and know, categorically, what technique you are going to use should you get into a situation when you take your wife/girlfriend etc out to the pictures later in the evening, your awareness allows that. Should your awareness drop and you get ambushed or find yourself in a match fight where sniper option is not an option then your support system comes into its own. Preparing for, and accepting, the latter is also a part of your game plan.

Of course, you should still practice all your other techniques and perhaps add to your main artillery as they improve.

Action triggers

An action trigger is a word or sentence used to 'trigger action'. When facing potential menace it is very often difficult to know how to initiate a physical response. One never quite knows the right time to attack or how to trigger that attack in a mind that does not want to become physical, even though it might be necessary. A key word or sentence will take away the decision making. Your chosen word/sentence will automatically initiate your attack. The trigger word/sentence can be any of your choosing, preferably it should be a submissive question, as opposed to a flat statement. This will serve the multi-purpose of switching off the opponent's adrenalin (submissiveness will intimate that you do not want to fight and switch off his fight or flight), brain engagement and action trigger. Also the submissive question subliminally intimates to your assailant that you wish to elongate conversation, where as shorter sentences, certainly single syllables, send the message that conversation is coming to an end.

Whilst the flat statement, ie, 'I don't want trouble', is submissive and can act as an action trigger it does not adequately engage the brain, because it does not demand an answer, neither does it suggest that you wish to elongate the conversation. So make your trigger a question. It can be any of your choosing, even an abstract question holds the multi-purpose, ie, 'how did the City get on today?' because of the confusion factor, after all, what has the 'City result' got to do with a guy asking for your wallet?

Of course this all works nicely in the context of the four D's, your multi-faceted question being Deception and Distraction before the Decision of fight or flight. If the antagonist proffers a question you may wish your trigger 'blurb' to be in the guise of an answer, or you may even feign deafness by saying, 'Sorry mate, I didn't hear you. What did you say?'

As long as it engages the brain. For maximum effect, launch your attack straight after the trigger question. You don't have to wait for an answer - ask the question and strike.

To make this more natural, practice your trigger question when hitting the bag or pads. The more natural it seems the more it is likely to engage the opponent. In a way the brain engagement is just a feint using psychology as opposed to physical technique, and it is the same engagement innately used by most attackers. Where a boxer, in the ring, may lead with a jab a street fighter will use dialogue and deception as his leading technique. This is why he is so successful at taking out even highly trained martial artists because he is using guile to prime force.

Support system

The support system should also be included in the game plan, as a back up just in case the main artillery fails or is not an option. Basically your support system is every technique and concept that you have ever learned - and they should each have been pressure tested. This will be enlarged upon in the next chapter.

Your game plan should be firstly to avoid, then, escape, third to use firm verbal dissuasion thirdly to initiate physical confrontation, and lastly to prepare for aftermath so that it does not impede your pre-fight ability.

When the 4th response is initiated you should utilise your main artillery (MA) technique, whatever that might be.

The majority of street attacks start at conversation range, this being punching range, so it would be logical to draw your MA attack from that range. There is little point in having a kick as your sniper option when kicking range is unlikely to occur. In your bid to attain the 'one punch kill' you will be looking to develop accuracy, speed and power, accuracy rising slightly above the other two necessities, because an accurate attack can be effective with minimal power and speed.

Worse case scenario (pre-post fight fear)

Many people bottle out before a confrontation because they get pre-post fight adrenalin, that is to say they worry about the consequences of their actions: police involvement, come backs etc. before the fight/encounter. So your game plan should also take into account the fact that there may be, and often is, a price to pay after the fact. Many a competent fighter has been destroyed because he has paid too much heed to consequence. I'm not saying that consideration should not be paid the consequence of one's actions: many times I have sat and worried about the possibility of badly hurting an opponent, even killing him, but not when he was in my face up some dark alley or on a nightclub door. That kind of hesitancy could (and has to some) prove fatal and has been the downfall of many an over-considerate person. The time to think about such things is now, not when a situation is imminent.

You have to look at aftermath and all that it contains before engaging in battle, police involvement, injury - to you or your opponent - death threats, house visits, come backs: these are all a part and parcel of defending yourself from life's malevolents, they cannot be separated - oh how I wish they could. The plain fact of the matter is the fighting, the physical side, is the easy part. It is dealing with the contributing factors that complicate matters. So to help you cope and stop pre-post-fight contemplation - as we have already stated when he's in your face it's too late to think about what happens afterwards - you should look at the worse case scenarios and deal with them before the fight. We are working, of course, on the premise that avoidance and escape is not a viable option or talking distance is running low and verbal dissuasion has not had the desired effect.

If my potential assailant has three bruiser brothers who may come back on me when I tear him a new arse then, before I fight with him I must first accept that I may have to fight them as a consequence. Once I have accepted this into the computation it can no longer be used as a leverage against me.

I faced one such lad who told me that his brothers would give me a visit if I beat him, I told him 'that's OK, I've already fought them all, they know where I am. Tell them to come on down'. A bemused look fell upon his face and then he found himself unexpectedly unconscious. He had beaten so many people with the reputation of his brothers, so many of his opponents had backed down because of his threats that, when I didn't, he didn't know what to do.

Many people use the threat of 'come back' as a way to psyche you out. It often masks the fact that they have not got the ability to 'walk the walk'. If, in your game plan, you have already accepted that there will be consequences then they can no longer be used against you.

A good example of this was the time I took out the leader of an infamous gang in Coventry - I put him in hospital for a week. I heard later through the grapevine that his gang had planned a revenge attack on me for the following weekend. They were going to visit my house and do the dirty deed in front of my family. I thought the idea was pretty bad form and spread the rumour very quickly that I had acquired the addresses of three gang leaders and that, after they had been to 'visit' me, I would visit all three addresses and destroy them in front of their families and that I'd make a point of visiting whilst they were having tea with their mum, 'so' I told them 'I'm ready whenever you are'.

Before I put the lad in hospital my game plan had included heavy come backs, I expected no less from such a notorious gang. I accepted that there would be a price to pay, more often than not people threaten until they are blue in the face but do not act on their threats. Talk is very cheap, but with these people I pretty much knew that there would be come backs.

My double bluff worked because although there were a couple of hundred people in this gang each one of them wondered whether it was their name and address that I had acquired so decided to give me a wide berth.

Police involvement is the same. Before an altercation I always accept that there may be involvement - even prison - post fight because the law in this country does not protect the people. So I deal with it beforehand, partly by accepting that they will come - if they, or anyone else, do not then that's a bonus - and partly by acquiring as a part of my game plan a good knowledge of the law and my rights to self defence within it and how to quote the law in my defence should I need to. As I have said before, people are often convicted for what they say and not what they do.

So before you act do your ram-uiy, exorcise the demons of aftermath from your mind by accepting the fact that, whatever the consequence, you'll handle it, then it is all down to your ability and the ability of the guy in front of you.

Chapter Five
Support system

The support system incorporates reaction as opposed to response; reaction being an unconscious act and response being a conscious act.

When someone walks towards you menacingly and you line him up you are responding, you consciously accept that he may be a threat and you respond to that threat by 'putting a fence around your factory' (to be detailed later). If he ambushes you then you react unconsciously, according to how well trained you are.

As I said earlier, if you are trained for reality, blood snot and all, then your reaction will usually be a good one. If, however, you have never trained for reality and you stop at the hurdle of pain, exhaustion, fear, blood etc then the chances are you will become a cowering heap of jelly.

So the support system should involve realistic training for the ambush, the match fight and what my friend and Sempai Dave Turton would call the 'what if syndrome'. What if this happens? What if that happens? What if you're wearing cumbersome clothes? What if your attacker is wearing a crash helmet? What if you get attacked in a swimming pool? What if you're sat behind a table in a pub? Stood on a slippery floor? etc. The list of possibilities can go on and on.

The 'what if syndrome' is an easy one to solve. Devise the most awkward situations that you can think of, recreate them in the dojo (the swimming pool may be a hard one) - or even on the street etc. and practice fighting, in those conditions, ambushes, match fights, line-ups etc.

We did a similar experiment at our club (this was one of Dave's ideas). Now, everyone at my club is used to fighting all out and at every range - but always in training clothes, so on this particular occasion I made everyone fight wearing wellington boots, very heavy clothing, tight cagoules or anoraks, gloves, basically I dressed them for a winter's day. To add to this we gave one person a couple of heavy shopping bags to carry - then told them to fight to KO or submission. What a difference it made! People were being choked out or smothered with their own cagoules, others were using the shopping bags as a weapon, others still were tripping up in the heavy wellingtons - and losing the fight as a consequence. Then we'd make them fight from a seated position or make them fight from a negative position (with their opponent already holding them in a head lock or pin etc).

Every variation was covered and all the fighting was to submission or KO. This kind of training develops the right reactions - that is to fight back ferociously as opposed to capitulating, and to adapt technique according to environment and clothing.

Circle training

Circle training is an excellent way in which to develop positive reaction to ambush attacks - not forgetting that the best reaction where possible is to avoid and escape - though it does need to be supported by a good repertoire of tested technique. It is not and cannot be 100% real because one actually does know that an attack is imminent, even though you may not know from whom or where.

The trainees/pupils form a circle on the mat. A volunteer steps into the middle (I always ask for, and encourage, volunteers so that the student is making the decision to step into adversity - after all I will not be there to push him in when it kicks off in the street). The volunteer is attacked intermittently by any one of the other students in the circle, at any time and with any technique - no control is used though bag/boxing gloves should be used to add minimal safety.

Sometimes I will restrict the attacks - rugger tackle/ right hook etc - or a certain range - kicking/grappling etc. Once the attack has been launched both combatants fight to a conclusion - KO/ submission etc. The person in the centre usually stays for two or three attacks and is then replaced by another volunteer.

With constant exposure to circle training you develop not only positive reaction but also workable technique because you are fighting against an attacker who has only one objective - to beat you. So if and when you beat him you know it is because the technique you used was a good one and not because your opponent let you win. You will also learn how to deal with the adrenal syndrome and a degree of pain - all necessary attributes in a real situation.

Match fighting

Match fighting is also an easy thing to prepare for - though it takes bottle in bags full to engage in match fighting - it is what most people do in the gym every training session, they spar. The only difference with true match fighting is that the sparring will not be at a designated range, rather it will be at any range that happens. Animal day is an excellent way of preparing for the match fight because there are very few rules and any range is permissible - also the fight is not over until one man gives in or is KO'd.

Animal day is good for many things, not least for showing you who you are and what you have got, but it is especially good for match fight preparation.

I think it is worth mentioning that match fighting is only a very small percentage of real fighting. The majority lies with line up fighting (three second fighting), though when/if a fight goes beyond three seconds a match fight is what it usually becomes - that's why it is a good idea to prepare for it, just in case. It is also important to mention the fact that, whether you agree or not, most fights that go beyond three seconds tend to end up on the floor so it is imperative that you learn to grapple for this eventuality.

Many practitioners that I have spoken to believe that their system is so good vertical that they do not need to prepare for horizontal. It's rather like someone saying that they are such good drivers that they do not need insurance or a seat belt because they are not going to crash. Generally when people say this it means one thing - they have no, or limited, experience of real fighting.

I had a European kickboxing champion come to my club to spar for an up and coming fight in Russia. He was a very capable lad and by the way he held himself I could tell that he was also very confident in his ability. Because we allow any range in the sparring at my club I thought it only right to give him fair warning,

'We allow any range at this club', I told him. 'How's your grappling?'

'Not very good' he said, honestly, 'but it don't matter, it ain't gonna get that far!'

He preceded to spar with my people and was on the floor more than the cleaner's mop. They could see that he was a good puncher and kicker so they immediately took him to his weakest range - on the ground.

I don't think people fully appreciate just how quickly situations can erupt in the real world and how fast a committed assailant will bridge the gap and be in your face.

People often talk about using a 'stop hit' - catching an opponent as he moves into attack - on a rushing assailant, saying that they would catch him with this technique and that technique as he moved forward - just like they do in the photo shoot self defence strips in the martial arts mags! Not in the real world matey, unless you're very lucky. In several hundred fights that kind of reaction has worked for me only once or twice. Fitting these 'stop hits' into a photo shoot is one thing, to do it with a real opponent who explodes at you like a bullet from a gun - not quite so easy.

I remember, even as a very young karataka, watching a fight in the local pub and thinking 'how the **ck do you fit martial art into that?' I innately knew that what I had would not work under real conditions unless I mad some radical changes in strategy and technique. Later, after acquiring some 'real' flight time I realised that the only way to fit it in was to do so just before the fight became physical-response/the sniper option - or, if the situation went beyond that to adapt what I had so that I could meet that 'in your face' grappling range with the ferocity and skill to out do my assailant.

I found that perception and awareness allowed me to utilise the sniper option in the vast majority of cases - and I trained to this end. I also realised that no matter how well thought out the game plan 'shit happens' so the ambush and match fight had to be addressed also.

In a way the ambush was easier than the sniper option because, as I have said, it is a subconscious reaction that is not contemplated/ thought over/dwelled upon or analysed. You just go with the flow. The sniper option, however, takes conscious thought and extreme control. You have to be proactive rather than reactive, you have to step forward and be first even though everything inside you seems to be pulling you back. We seem, in this day and age, to be indoctrinated with the 'no first attack philosophy'. We are taught from youth not to attack first, so, to completely reverse this ethos means reversing the way we think and subsequently the way we train. Everything we do in the martial arts seems to start with defence and is then followed by a counter attack: 'when the opponent strikes with this move we block and counter attack'. Or even better still make the blocking technique so hard that it injures and thus discourages our attackers. And so to this end we practice defence and counter against a multitude of different attacks, most of which are attacks of our own design that no one is ever likely to use, all executed from a safe range, (in some styles/schools a ridiculously safe range) then we wonder what went wrong when reality kicks our arse.

After making a few early mistakes and ending up grappling on the floor with some lowlife trying to make me a hat out of a beer glass - and the onlookers turning their noses up and saying 'I thought he was a supposed to be a Karate man' as though karate has failed if you go to ground - I wondered just why that distance was lost so quickly and one ended up fighting on the floor even before you realised that a fight was on the cards? I did a little study on this and I watched maybe in excess of a few thousand fights and this is my conclusion:

If you look at someone like Linford Christie, he can cover 100 metres in under 10 seconds, that's about 30 feet a second. Now if he can cover 30 feet a second how fast could he cover two feet? Three, four even five feet? Probably in the blink of an eye. So when you face a guy in the street, loaded with the human turbo drive adrenalin, how long is it going to take him to cover the distance at which one argues? Not very long. So quickly, in fact, that after the fight you can't even remember how the distance was lost.

Line ambush

A great way to demonstrate this is to practice line ambush. Not only is this a good way to develop fast reaction it is also an excellent way to enlighten those who are still not convinced.

Stand one student in front of a line of other students. The guy at the front should stand in a natural stance, the way you might stand in a pub or at the bus stop, facing the line. He should wear bag gloves (as opposed to boxing gloves).

The first student in the line facing him should move forward until he can touch him with an outstretched arm (about 19"-24") then, whenever he is ready he should rush forward and try to rugger tackle the guy at the front to the ground. From the natural stance, arms by side, the guy at the front should try to stop him from grabbing with any technique he wishes to use - with no restriction on control - if he can he should try and knock his opponent out, this will encourage realism on both sides. Once the fighters reach a clinch situation on the ground they should break and the next guy in the line attack. Change around and place different people at the front of the line.

When everyone has had a go extend the distance between attacker and defender until, eventually, there is a gap of about ten feet.

This will show you just how hard it is to hit a man who is rushing forward and also just how difficult it can be avoiding grappling range.

Grab reaction

Another valid training method for the ambush is grab training, that is you allow your opponent to grab you from different positions and angles and then defend accordingly. This is not a big part of my own training because I tend to use the 'fence around the factory' defence, which makes it very difficult for an opponent to grab. However, as I said earlier, we all make mistakes, even monkeys fall out of trees, so every scenario has to be addressed.

I haven't got a great deal of belief in locks and levers when someone has grabbed you. More often than not if someone does not want to let go of you they won't, unless you can cause a reaction that will force them to let go, like a poke in the eye or a punch on the nose. In theory the pain of a lock should force an opponent out of a grab; in reality it usually does not. When someone grabs you within a conflict they are usually charged with panic. I remember head butting a guy who had hold of my shirt, three times, as hard as I could. I hit him so hard that I laid him out and later he had to be taken to hospital with concussion but it still did not release his panic grip. He had gripped my shirt so hard that when he fell he ripped it clean off my back (after the hospital treated him for concussion and a severed finger tip he had to have an operation to remove my shirt from his fingers).

I also read about a Ju-Jitsu guy who tried to hold an assailant in the street with a very painful arm lock that had had everyone 'tapping out' in the dojo, the guy head butted the Ju-Jitsu man so hard that he KO'd him, then ran off cradling a broken arm. This is not to say that they cannot work, just try not to be too shocked when an uncompliant assailant does not fall over and play dead.

In grab reaction training it is important to instil, in the grabber & grabbed, a sense of realism. People in real situations rarely grab for the sake of grabbing, they grab to add leverage to a strike or they grab to pull a victim to the floor. So to make the exercise more realistic the grabber should grab and then try to wrestle the opponent to the floor or hit him or whatever, there should be no compliance (except for when one first learns technique). Again this kind of exercise should make the whole scenario an enlightening experience and unrealistic techniques will rise to the top of the broth leaving you with only those that will work.

Chapter Six
The fence

Priming - putting a fence around your factory

When the police talk about self protection the key word is 'target hardening', that is, making yourself a hard target by means of placement and awareness of environment and the enemy. When I talk about the physical aspect of self protection I am always working on the premise that, for whatever reason, a situation has gone beyond this and reached dire straits and the possibility of escape is no longer an option or the option has been lost.

As I said earlier in the book, the winner and loser in most situations is usually determined by what happens pre-fight as opposed to in-fight. Most situations start at conversation range, this being talking or hand shake distance. If this is mismanaged it degenerates rather quickly to vertical grappling range and then ground fighting - not a good place to be if you don't know ground fighting or are faced by more than one opponent. Whilst conversation distance is not a chosen range - most people feel safer at about four or five feet - it can be maintained so that it does not degenerate further into grappling by 'putting a fence around your factory'.

If you had a factory that you wanted to protect from robbers the most sensible thing to do would be to place a fence around it to make it a hard target so that a potential robber has got to get past that fence before he can even think about attacking the factory. Whilst the fence might not keep him out indefinitely it will make his job decidedly harder. Rather like a boxer who constantly flicks a jab into his opponent's face, even if that jab does not hurt his opponent it still keeps him at bay, and if his opponent wants to employ his

Knock Out blow he first has to find a way past his opponent's jab. To the boxer the jab is the fence around his factory.

In self protection the fence around your factory is your lead hand, placed in that all important space between you and your antagonist to maintain a safe gap.

Like the factory fence the lead hand will not keep an aggressor at bay forever - just long enough for you to initiate an escape or a pre-emptive attack - but it will place you in charge, even though your aggressor may not know it. Placed correctly the lead hand will not only maintain a safe gap but it will also disable the attacker's armoury - right and left hand techniques/ head butt etc - (though he may not know it on a conscious level he will instinctively realise that, until that fence has been removed or by-passed, his techniques have no clear way through).

Sensory tentacle

The lead hand should be held in a non aggressive way (see illus.) and should not touch the aggressor unless he makes a forward movement and tries to bridge the gap between you and he. It acts as a sensory guide to your aggressor's intentions: if he moves forward he will touch the fence and set your alarm bells ringing. This forward movement should be checked so as to maintain the safe range by using the palm of the lead hand on the aggressor's chest. Don't hold the touch as this may be seen by your assailant on a conscious level as a controlling movement (whilst of course it is a controlling action it's better at this stage that the aggressor does not feel that you are in control). This will force him to knock your hand away or grab your wrist and possibly cause him to attack you prematurely, so as soon as you have checked him return the lead hand to its stand-by position.

One of the final subliminal pre-pre-cursors to an aggressor's attack is distance close down. If he tries to bridge the gap that you are maintaining it is usually because he is making his final preparations for assault, so if he does move forward and touch the fence you should, as well as checking range, be getting ready to attack preemptively or suffer the consequences should he break down the fence. In my opinion the maximum amount of times that a potential attacker should be allowed to touch the 'fence' is twice - after that you've got big problems and will probably end up in a match fight situation or on the floor with a crowd around you, depending up on the calibre of fighter you are facing. Every time the attacker touches the fence the danger doubles.

The 'fence' should look and feel natural. This will come with practice: if it does not and the attacker notices it on a conscious level he will try to knock it away and bridge the gap. Ideally the 'fence' should look like you are using your hands to talk ('talking hands' as my friend Mourice Teague calls it).

A professional may notice the 'fence' no matter how well you disguise it and try using deceptive dialogue or body language to bring the 'fence' down, once down he will act. This often entails telling you that he does not want trouble, or that he 'just wants to talk', he may ask directions, the time, your name anything to disarm you enough to lower the fence. An experienced fighter will offer to shake hands to get rid of the fence or try to close the gap by putting his arm around you in a pally kind of way - don't have any of it. If there is the slightest chance of threat then don't let anyone touch you. A good fighter will only need one shot once the fence is down so keep it up. If he still persists in coming forward and you do not feel ready to strike, or indeed are not even sure that a strike is called for, don't hesitate to back-up the 'check' with a firm verbal fence; 'Just stay where you are'.

With the modern enemy the rule of thumb is 'if his lips are moving he's lying' so don't believe a word that he says. If he still persists in coming forward then he has given you the 'go'. Having said all that, if the potential attacker has already made his intentions obvious by asking you for your wallet or threatening you then there is nothing to contemplate, you should 'go' the first time the touches the 'fence'.

Range finder

The fence also acts as a range finder - many trained fighters misjudge the distance of their attacks in a real situation because the range is foreign to them by touching the opponent with the lead hand before initiating your attack you can judge the exact distance, this enabling you a more accurate and solid shot.

Action trigger

If and when you have decided to initiate an attack the lead hand also acts as a physical action trigger, you touch the opponent with the lead hand - find the range - and bounce off the touch using it to trigger your attack. This should be coupled by the verbal action trigger detailed earlier.

Multiple attackers

The 'fence' can also be used to maintain the range and even position of multiple attackers. But this is tantamount to fighting on more than one front, and it is very difficult to maintain the range of more than one attacker so a speedy decision to attack or escape should always be sought.

The fence can be constructed in any way you choose as long as it blocks the gap and looks inoffensive. You can use a 'stop fence' by placing the palm of the lead hand to/in front of the opponent, but this will bring the control to a conscious level and may catalyse alarm in the opponent - where possible it is best to control him without him knowing it.

Here are a couple of suggested fences

The pleading fence (PF)

This is a nice fence because it is submissive and inoffensive but it blocks range perfectly. It also leaves the fingers ideally placed for an eye attack should it be needed. It is often best to underline the fence with firm dissuasive dialogue, 'look, just keep away from me, I don't want trouble,' or a more assertive 'stay where you are - don't come any closer'.

Submissiveness is ideal if you have decided that you are going to employ a pre-emptive attack or you are using the deception to escape, it will mentally disarm your opponent making him an easy target. It has, however, a bad point: many attackers will see submissiveness as a meal ticket to an easy victim and spur on their assault, which is OK if you are setting the trap but not so good if you are not expecting it. Personally I use the submissive approach quite a lot because it really does disarm the opponent and give you a clear line for the sniper option, whereas other times I will use an assertive, even aggression fence, to psyche out the opponent.

Assertiveness can be a good thing and a bad thing. If the attacker thinks that you are confident it may cause him to abort his intended attack. After all, 'when ignorance is mutual confidence is king', but if he is committed to attacking you no matter what, your assertiveness may trigger his aggression and you may lose the element of surprise.

Having spent a lot of time working with and controlling violent people I have learned to judge the right time for assertiveness and the right time for submissiveness. Not everyone will be able to do this so - if you have to choose and there is no other way, use submissiveness to disarm and then attack and run, or use firm (but not aggressive) or submissive - verbal dissuasion.

Both hands are placed in front of you, palms facing the attacker and several inches away from him but not touching.

The staggered fence (SF)

Similar to the PF with palms facing forward but with the hands staggered by about twelve inches. The hand at the back would be the ideal one used to attack though with practice the lead hand would be ideally placed for a finger strike to the eyes.

The exclamation fence (EF)

The hands, palms upward, are held as though in exclamation, the lead left hand pushed forward as fence and the right hand, cocked to strike, to your own right hand side (left if reversed).

The verbal fence

The verbal fence is an excellent tool if you can see menace on its way in and works well pre-fight, in-fight and post fight. I have used it successfully many times. This extract from my book *Watch My Back* exemplifies a post-fight fence rather well.

The fight with 'the karate kid' had been on the cards for several months. I'd tried to avoid it but was unable. I pick up the situation as it reached its conclusion - the post-fight fence comes in at the end of the fight when one of his friends becomes involved; (this was a match fight by the way).

"I'd spent two months trying to avoid this situation and was fed up with trying, I had no more chances left in my 'chance bag'.

As the karate kid got closer his face began to grimace and I sensed he was going to strike at any moment.

'BANG!' Almost in slow motion, I hooked my right fist onto his advancing jaw, pushing it backwards, shaking his grey matter into the realms of unconsciousness. As he fell I volleyed his face and he spiralled, like movie strobe. I kicked him so hard that it hurt my foot. I felt hate leaving my body; he landed face down and forlorn on the cruel, black tarmac of defeat. Many people were watching, so I thought I'd give them a display, not for exhibitionism, nor fun, nor ego, I just wanted to take out a little insurance. Making the onlookers (mostly his mates) think that I was an animal would, in the future, ensure that they did not tangle with me. It's what the Chinese call 'killing a chicken to train a monkey'.

'Kiaaa,' I screamed as I brought an axe kick onto the body of my sleeping quarry. To the onlooker, it probably looked barbaric, (which is how I wanted it to look), but in reality the kick was empty, I pulled it on impact, just as I had a thousand times in training.

The man with the weasel face (the karate kid's mate) ran at me, from the crowd of onlookers, with ill intent and I stopped him in his tracks with a lash of my tongue (the verbal fence).

'GER OUT 'F MY ****ING FACE BEFORE I DESTROY YA!'

I pointed at him to underline my resolve. He stopped like an insect on fly paper."

The Psychological fence

The psychological fence is a fighter's reputation or confident/ aggressive gait - this places an invisible fence around you that only the very brave will try to pass.

The negative psychological fence

Deliberately dropping the physical or psychological fence by pretending to be scared or unthreatening can draw the opponent forward onto your intended attack - he walks into a trap.

Unlike the varying genres of physical fence the verbal fence is best aggressive - the more so the better. It has to pierce the opponent's subconscious and register danger with the brain - thus causing an adrenal reaction in him that, hopefully, he will mistake for fear.

In America they have a saying in the prisons 'Give me five feet', meaning keep at least five feet away from me, five feet being the distance at which they feel they are relatively safe. This only works if you're perceptive/aware enough to spot menace at a very early stage. More often than not a fight will come through an argument or some kind of aggressive verbal so the five feet rule is already lost and the physical fence comes into play.

If you are using the verbal fence you must, as I have said, be very firm/even aggressive,

'Stay where you are, don't come any closer, stay!'

This would be underlined by placing your lead hand in front of you in a stop sign.

This can even work in-fight if someone tries to attack you whilst you are fighting/defending yourself. I have been grappling on the floor with one opponent when his mate has tried to join in against me. Noticing this I used an in-fight fence by telling the guy that if he joined in I was going to batter him afterwards - he quickly changed his mind.

On the one hand the physical fence will control range and prime your attack. On the other hand, if you are not sure whether to strike or not, the fence allows you time to maintain a relatively safe range whilst you plan a course of action, bearing in mind that decision making this late in the game is not a good thing, though sometimes it is unavoidable.

As I've previously mentioned, Sir Winston Churchill once said that occasionally people stumble upon the truth - and then get back up and wander off as though nothing happened. The truth is, in the three second fight, the 'fence' is one of the best, if not the best, little techniques available for controlling the early stages of an altercation, but it is so simple that many people often fail to see its importance. It is too easy and they are looking for something more advanced or fantastic. To be honest the advanced stuff, the fantastic stuff, only works in the James Bond films. The fence should therefore become the bedrock of all your physical self protection work - ignore it at your own peril.

Chapter Seven
The Attack

The attack is your chosen main artillery technique and whilst many techniques should be practised and perfected, one or two, the ones that work best for you, should be taken to one side and isolated - these will be the techniques used in your sniper option.

There is no sense in beating about the bush and saying that main artillery can be taken from any range because they can't. If punching range is the one most often given in a real situation then that is where the main artillery should be drawn from. Having said that I always think it is wise to have one or two very strong techniques at every range, after all a chain is only as strong as its weakest link.

So, hand techniques are the order of the day, and there is little point in manufacturing another range when the one you are in is the most clinical anyway. Kicking and grappling range are far from clinical. They are, at best, elongated ranges where it usually takes several blows or seconds to finish an adversary as opposed to the split second it can take to finish a fight with a good hand technique. Punching range is also a very mobile range and a good puncher can move through several opponents in as many seconds. This would be very difficult with kicking range - kicks are better employed as a finishing technique to a prostrate opponent - and almost impossible with grappling range, which is better suited to the match fighter.

I will list a few techniques that I have, and do, use but, basically, any short range hand technique, as long as it is a finishing technique, will suffice. I would keep clear of time wasting and superfluous technique. Once you get this far you may have one chance and one chance only - don't waste it. Once the opportunity has gone it may never present itself again. Your attack should be a destroying technique that hits your opponent like a steam train, not a sillyflicky back fist that might make his eyes water. If you want to do that you'd be better employed reading him an extract from Love Story.

Trapping/jamming and the likes are also unlikely to have any relevance here. Unless you allow someone to touch or grab you then a trap can be followed by a devastating head butt or hand strike. Once a fight becomes live nothing stays still for long and the concept of flowing through a series of trapping movements is not a sound one. If you beg to differ then I respect your opinion but please don't try to convince me. Have an animal day at your own club and see for yourself. When you watch someone like the brilliant Rick Young teach trapping it makes you realise what a valid part of your armoury it can be. But even Rick will probably tell you it is an incidental range used to back up main artillery. Basic trapping therefore is a valid - though very small - part of the support system. A fight goes from talking distance to 'in your face' in the blink of a eye.

People often ask me what is the best means of physical defence and I always reply 'learn to hit ****ing hard', and that's the bottom line. Learn how to hit very very hard and you'll come out of most situations on top, but please learn to do it from the right range. It's one thing being able to hit hard from a comfortable range and from a guard position or perhaps even using combination to build momentum and power but how well will you fare when the distance you are used to is halved and you have to punch from a no-guard position? It's a completely different ball game so it is important to train your techniques as close to reality as possible so that when you make the step from dojo to street that step is not such a big one. If you are used to compliance in training you've got a very big shock coming to you when the shit hits the fan.

In the vast majority of situations I have been involved in I have used a left lead 'fence' to set up a right handed punch - sometimes a cross, sometimes a hook. My base was, and is, usually always a very small left lead forty-five degree stance and I always ask a question before I strike. Others I have worked with preferred a left lead stance and a right hand fence punching with a left hook off the lead leg, others still favoured a left lead fence from a left lead stance and attacked with a pummelling head butt.

For those that prefer it, the lead hand or reverse hand finger strike is also a good 'stopping technique'.

The following illustrations are some of the favoured.

The exclamation fence . . . right cross

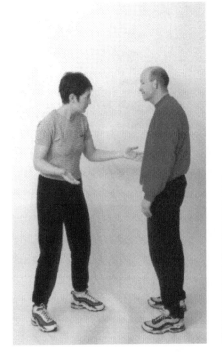 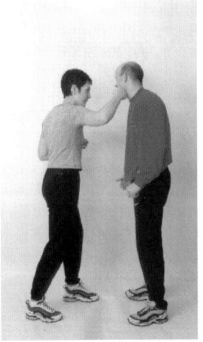

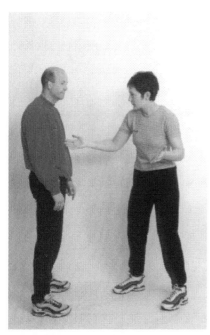 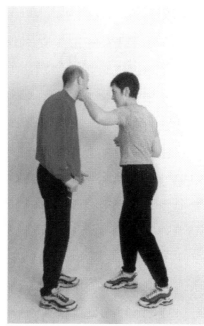

The reverse hand fence . . . left hook

Passive fence . . . head butt

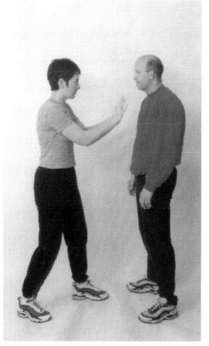 

As a final point on attack, don't ever pull your technique. If a situation has become so bad that you are forced to hit someone to protect yourself then they deserve everything they get. Pulling your technique is the quickest way to the graveyard, so either attack all out or do not attack at all. The only exception to this rule is if you are very experienced and feel you can judge the potency of your attacker. I was often faced with people that were not enough of a threat to demand a good hiding so I would use an adrenalin switch (see *Dead or Alive*) to psyche them out and thus beat them without coming to arms. This, though, takes a lot of experience and unless you are very experienced don't take the chance.

It is also my recommendation that, once you have hit your opponent, you make good your escape. The only time you need to finish off an opponent is when he is still a threat. If he is not then there is no need (I know this contradicts some of the things I have said in Watch My Back but that [bouncing] again is a different arena where many rules have to be broken to keep the peace - long term). I have seen many people go for a finish when a finish was not necessary - and lose as a consequence. Use the distraction of your attack to make good an escape - that's my advice if the situation is a self defence one. If it is a fight situation you may need to stay and finish off.

Chapter Eight
Aftermath, Law
– the second enemy

By Peter Consterdine 8th Dan EKGB

I thought it apt to include this chapter, taken from a newsletter by Peter to British Combat Association members in January 96 (The British Combat Ass. is a self defence association that Peter and I run together) in light of the recent bad publicity that reality training has received from the police and the media. We all have to be held responsible for our actions with regard to self defence but more than that we have to look out for the second enemy in today's society - the law. Many people are convicted in self defence situations not for what they have done but for what they have said in their police statements - post fight.

To attain realism one has to train for realism. When we do we are slated by our peers, the uninitiated, for being bruisers, philistines, animals etc because we do not exclude socially unacceptable technique from our syllabus and because we are not afraid to promote what is needed to successfully survive a violent encounter. We are made to feel like the scum of the earth because of our empirically based beliefs. I will leave Peter to better describe the hypocrisy that abounds - GT.

I'll start this article with apologies to the many serving police officers out there who are conscientiously trying to uphold the law - the following is not directed at them, rather at senior police and home office management.

Just recently one of the clubs registered to the BCA has come under the spotlight in his area for running an abridged version of Geoff's 'animal day'. He's actually only been doing it at night, but calling it 'animal night' doesn't quite have the same ring. Unfortunately he's drawn attention from both the local police and news media, who are both endeavouring to close him down and develop a prosecution for organising any injuries which students might inflict on each other. As we know, with the exception of a few bloody noses, no serious injuries ever occur during realistic training events, but the impression they give is always worse than the actuality.

I am always ambivalent over police matters, particularly when it comes to self defence. My sympathies are very much with them regarding their own problems on the street and during any year I instruct many police officers in 'practical protection issues'. What I can't come to terms with is the hypocrisy which attends senior police attitudes with regards to the general public's equal wish to be as capable as any police officer wishes to be in his or her own defence.

Over the past few years we have seen police officers, quite rightly, 'harden' themselves to increasing acts of violence. Stab vests, quick cuffs, side handled batons, expanding metal coshes, long batons and now CS gas, have all been trialed and adopted so as to give a police officer an even chance with the villains that roam the streets. Decades of ad-hoc and ineffective police self defence training is now being overturned in favour of a co-ordinated instruction strategy which combines the use of all this modern equipment in a common way and also to include unarmed control and restraint techniques.

A recent article in Police Review entitled 'fighting talk' extolled the virtue of the Strathclyde Constabulary's 5 day self defence training programme. An inspector, Alex Hossack is quoted as saying 'society is changing and we have to adapt to meet these changes'. This statement was supported, statistically by the fact that the force had more than 50% of operational officers assaulted in 1993 and a PC tragically stabbed to death in Glasgow in 1994.

The course is unique in that it runs over 5 days and the operational 'down time' to the force in lost manpower is tremendous, but reflects the growing necessity for self defence training. It reflects the very seriousness of the situation out there on the streets.

The point is those are the same streets that we're on, not just our police, so it's all right for them to 'gear up' to a worsening situation, but when we train for reality as situations demand out there, we walk closer to that indistinct line on the floor than if we step over we break the law, seemingly even in our training.

This is compounded by the fact that the police as an authority, will always go to great lengths to disguise and confuse as to what the law says about self defence.

When talking about training for reality, even this is a problem for the police with regard to old, out of date attitudes. An article in Feb. 95 headed 'Checks on Self Defence Classes' dealt with the injuries to officers in self defence classes and whether instructors were adequately trained due to the high level of injuries. It highlighted a report about one training establishment which came under criticism for a high level of injuries and the report called for the head of the centre to report. He simply stated that the level of injuries affected the seriousness which his staff attached to safety and also that they were meticulous, in any case, in recording all the injuries. What eventually came out was that they would always have a problem in balancing safe dojo practices with training for reality. It's the old problem of breaking eggs and making omelettes etc.

That's all 'animal day' or any other realistic training programme hopes to achieve. Forget the title – it's just sensational to draw attention to its cause. It's simply training for reality which necessarily includes the use of every weapon in one's armoury, be it biting, head butts, chokes, strangles etc, but all in a controlled way.

Don't ever start to think that such things as biting are illegal or not allowed at law in the perceived 'Queensbury' rules of the street. I quote from the Metropolitan Police bodyguard course for their officers:

Item 7 - Maximum Force Potential

'Concentration of the greatest proportion of your strength against the most vulnerable area of your opponent's body will achieve the best results'.

Controlled reaction

'The degree of attack will dictate the amount of force required to stop it. There is no need, under these circumstances, to protect the VIP's image or consider public opinion. You do not have the time, further - no serious complaint is likely to be entertained where an armed assailant is seriously injured by police warding off a vicious attack on them or their VIP.'

The manual goes on to talk about vulnerable points and states, 'the body has many anatomically weak areas, but only a few can be termed truly vulnerable in the context of unarmed combat.

Primary Points

The eyes, the throat, the testicles.

The manual goes on to talk about combining these areas of attack and that two at one time are better than one. As we know, strikes to the throat can kill quite easily. Of singular importance in all this however is the list of 'Potential Body Weapons'.

The following are useful in attack/defence.

HEAD - to attack the face, nose etc.

ELBOW- to attack kidneys, stomach etc.

TEETH- to attack nose, cheek, or neck (jugular vein).

Note: in view of the diseases which are known to be blood transferred, the teeth should only be used as an absolute last ditch method of obtaining release.

Never use your fist on a hard body surface.

Always when striking attempt to strike through the target: look beyond and attempt to hit it. You will then disperse all the force into the target area.

All the above quotes are exactly as presented in the manual and it's interesting to note that the only caveat on biting is in relation to the problems of transferring diseases, not the injuries that may be suffered.

All the above, if occasion demands, is allowed and legitimate and if biting, gouging and head butts etc are all that's left to you to possibly save your life or prevent serious injury to you or others, then the law relating to us is no different than the law of self defence for police officers.

Whilst the police are, at last, making it would seem, some serious in-roads into good effective and tactical kit and reality of training, the average man and woman on the street cannot be forgotten.

If you ask a police officer whose responsibility is the safety of individuals they will answer 'the person themselves'. The police are not there to look after your safety - you are.

In any police manual issued to the prominent and wealthy on 'personal security', you will read the same principle stated on every occasion which is that 'the individual is responsible for his or her own security'.

So if that's the case - let us get on with it. We will stay within the law, but we'll work up to the very limit of it in both training and in actuality.

Eventually, the ultimate test of one's legal correctness of action is not in someone else's view, nor in the hands of the police, but rests with the Crown Prosecution Service, who are responsible for eventually prosecuting. Their track record to date is less than admirable, prosecuting only 50% of police cases submitted to them and 'plea bargaining' down to trivia for crimes committed by violent and experienced criminals. Even then, facing a prosecution, you still have your defence through the courts. At the time of assault I'm not going to think about the consequences and I'll definitely take my chance with the system.

Another quote that I think is relevant to indicate changing social statement that 'Everyone has been relying on the traditional image of the British bobby and the weight the uniform carried, but it doesn't provide the degree of help it did in the past - we were concerned to get something that really works for officers' - Alex Hossack.

Well let me tell you, we're concerned to get something that really works for the average person who faces violence and assault and muggings and who hasn't even got a uniform to impress, whether out of date or not.

TIMES HAVE CHANGED - control has effectively been lost on the street and the 'animals' are out of the zoo. It's not just media hype - it's fact. It is also a fact that more Met. police officers have been killed since 1990 than in the NYPD. There is some hope as the home secretary had announced a review of policy on victims of crime who use the right to self defence.

'It is in the interests of no one, not the police, nor the CPS and certainly not the public, for criminal proceedings to be started against those who have dome no more than was reasonable to defend themselves, their family and their property.'
Michael Howard

WE'LL SEE!
Peter Consterdine

SELF DEFENCE AND THE LAW

Before I delve into the histrionics of the law and how you the victim stand within it, I must say this. As important as the law may be, you would be foolish to contemplate such a thought when an assault on your person is imminent. To think of such things will cause indecision which begets defeat. One second of indecision can mean the difference between defending yourself successfully and getting battered/raped/robbed.

'Better to be judged by twelve, than carried by six.'

The law is often even negligent with its own officers.

Coventry Evening Telegraph. January 13, 1995.

"Police watchdogs are demanding a hardline court crackdown on drunken street yobs behind the rising tide of attacks on beat bobbies.

They want an end to so-called plea bargaining between lawyers, which leads to thugs facing 'watered down' charges.

The plea for action from Warwickshire police authority is a direct reaction to the 50% surge in the number of attacks on officers last year.

A total of 377 days were lost through sickness as 169 male, 26 female and 16 special police officers were reported as too badly hurt to work.

Chief Constable Peter Joslin admitted officers were left frustrated and annoyed when cases of assault against them were dropped in exchange for guilty pleas to other more or less serious charges.

He said, 'Most of the attacks are alcohol related. Only last weekend an officer was assaulted twice in one night, once with a billiard ball in a sock.

'We are seen more and more as fair game, but it is as much a problem with society as anything else.'"

Talk to any policeman or read any text on law and from out of the maelstrom of labyrinthine paragraphs and sub-paragraphs one word, 'reasonable' will stand out. An assault upon a person who is attacking, or even about to attack you, must show 'reasonable' force if it is to be deemed lawful. The dictioned word states: 'In accordance with reason. Not extreme or excessive'.

Section 3, Criminal Law Act 1967 states: 'A person may use such force as is 'reasonable' in the circumstances, in the prevention of crime'.

March 1993, Wakefield, West Yorkshire.

"A man who bit a chunk of another man's nose walked free from the crown court after a jury decided he had acted in self defence."

Even a serious wounding upon an adversary maybe excusable if it is occasioned reasonably in the circumstances, and all the more justifiable in court, (though not essential), if the person claiming self defence demonstrates that at the time of the assault/attempted assault, he did not want to fight. Even the pre-emptive strike is tolerated in law, if the person claiming self defence can again show that he was in imminent danger of assault.

"Attorney General's Reference No. 2 of 1983. An individual can protect himself in advance from attack, for example by arming himself or making a bomb, and this can constitute self defence."

Honest belief

If you can say that you honestly believed that an attack upon your person was imminent then a pre-emptive attack can be employed and self defence claimed - but the threat has to be obvious. If, for instance, your assailant is stood at the other side of the road and you walked across and hit him, that would not be seen as self defence and your pre-emptive attack would be outside of the law.

This may be demonstrated in law by the person claiming self defence telling the police or courts, (if applicable), for example, that the antagonist shouted profanities at him and then moved aggressively toward him, forcing him to attack first. Again it helps if you can demonstrate that at the time you did not want to fight. Of course, the pre-emptive strike must be justified. If, for instance, your antagonist/potential antagonist has his hands in his pockets at the time of your pre-emptive strike, your actions might well be seen as unlawful. If you knock the person to the ground using reasonable force, to all intents and purposes, a further strike to the said person would be classed as unreasonable force, and therefore, unlawful (unless he was trying to get back up to attack you). This also ties in nicely with my recommendation to 'hit and run'.

In brief and to sum up, the law states, in the case of self defence of property or of another, (Butterworth - Police Law), self defence and the defence of property or of another are common law defences. However, a person who acts in defence of himself, or another, or of property, is invariably acting in the prevention of crime in which case he also has the defence under the Criminal Law Act 1967, Section 3. For practical purposes, the terms of both the common law and the statutory defences are identical in their requirements.

The issue of self defence as an excuse for a non-fatal offence against the person has been summarised extremely well by the court of appeal. The court said that it was both good law and good sense that a person who is attacked may defend himself, but that in doing so, he may only do what is reasonably necessary.

The test of whether or not the force is reasonable is an objective one, but it is assessed on the facts as the person concerned believed them to be. It is also important, but not essential, that a person claiming self defence demonstrated that he did not want to fight.

Again, I must re-emphasise that too much regard to 'how you stand within the law' could prove detrimental.

The time to think about such things is either before (not actually prior to attack, rather in the controlled arena when looking at worse case scenario), as a part of your game plan, or afterwards when (if), the police become involved.

Basically, if you pre-emptively attack an attacker and then make good your escape, which is what I recommend, you should be safe in the eyes of the law as long as you claim self defence and quote the law. As I have already said, people are often convicted for what they say as opposed to what they do, so if self defence is your aim, even your business, then make it your duty to understand completely how you stand within the law.

As a final note: the law differs from country to country, though most recognise the right to 'self defence'. The foregoing chapter should be used as a rule of thumb and not as actual fact.

For more details contact your local police station.

Conclusion

There is not a lot more to say that I have not already said. What is most important and stands repeating is that three second fighting, match fighting and ambush fighting are all different and demand different methods of training and defence. I can categorically state that, unless you are completely unaware in which case every situation will be a virtual ambush fight, most situations will fall into the three second fighter category. The most important three seconds are not those in-fight but those pre-fight. These are the ones that usually determine the winner and the loser, so learn the rituals of attack, train for pre-emptiveness and above all train for realism.

Thanks.

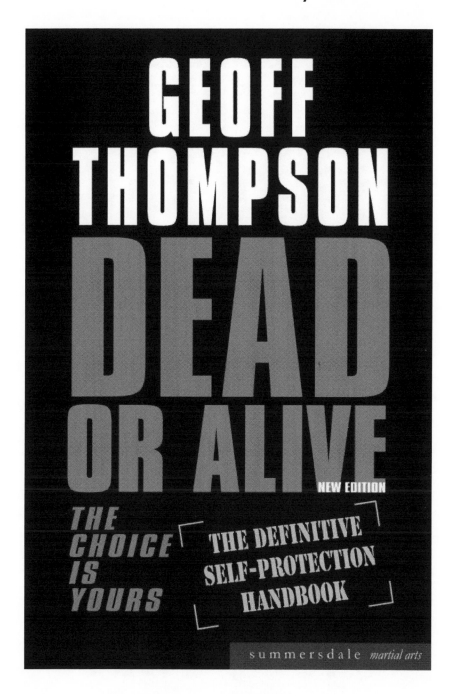

GEOFF
THOMPSON

DEAD
OR ALIVE

NEW EDITION

THE
CHOICE
IS
YOURS

THE DEFINITIVE
SELF-PROTECTION
HANDBOOK

summersdale *martial arts*

THE
PAVEMENT
ARENA

ADAPTING COMBAT MARTIAL ARTS TO THE STREET

GEOFF
THOMPSON

SUMMERSDALE

GEOFF THOMPSON

BESTSELLING
AUTHOR OF
WATCH MY BACK

'A compelling read' FHM

RED MIST

By the same author:

THE ELEPHANT AND THE TWIG

The Art Of Positive Thinking

14 Golden Rules to Success and Happiness

GEOFF THOMPSON

author of *Watch My Back* and *Fear*

SUMMERSDALE

www.geoffthompson.com

www.summersdale.com